Black Girl in Love (with Herself)

DISCARD

A GUIDE TO SELF-LOVE, HEALING, AND
CREATING THE LIFE YOU TRULY DESERVE

Black Girl in Love (with Herself)

TREY ANTHONY

HAY HOUSE, INC.
Carlsbad, California • New York City
London • Sydney • New Delhi

Published in the United States by: Hay House, Inc.: www.hayhouse
.com® • **Published in Australia by:** Hay House Australia Pty. Ltd.: www
.hayhouse.com.au • **Published in the United Kingdom by:** Hay House
UK, Ltd.: www.hayhouse.co.uk • **Published in India by:** Hay House Publishers India: www.hayhouse.co.in

Project editor: Melody Guy
Cover design: The Book Designers
Interior design: Julie Davison

Library of Congress Cataloging-in-Publication Data

Names: Anthony, Trey, author.
Title: Black girl in love (with herself) : a guide to self-love, healing,
    and creating the life you truly deserve / Trey Anthony.
Identifiers: LCCN 2020039175 | ISBN 9781401960261 (trade paper-
back) | ISBN
    9781401960278 (ebook)
Subjects: LCSH: African American women--Psychology. | African
American
    women--Life skills guides. | Self-realization in women. | Self-es-
teem in
    women.
Classification: LCC E185.86 .A55 2021 | DDC 305.48/896073--dc23
LC record available at https://lccn.loc.gov/2020039175

Tradepaper ISBN: 978-1-4019-6026-1
E-book ISBN: 978-1-4019-6027-8
Audiobook ISBN: 978-1-4019-6028-5

10 9 8 7 6 5 4 3 2 1
1st edition, January 2021

Printed in the United States of America

SUSTAINABLE
FORESTRY
INITIATIVE
Certified Chain of Custody
Promoting Sustainable Forestry
www.sfiprogram.org
SFI-01268
SFI label applies to the text stock

To my mom, Angela Senior, who has shown me what it means to get back up. Thank you for always allowing me to tell my version of my truth and being open to hearing it.

To my family. For always giving me something to write about. I love you.

To my grannies. Enid and Daphne, I know you're both looking down smiling. I feel your presence every day.

To my friends. The ones who hold me down at all times. Sis wouldn't have made it here without you.

To my beautiful son, Kai. You're my "why." The reason I didn't give up. You are the constant light in the darkest days. I love you. Thank you for choosing me to be your mummy.

God/Universe: May I continue to do your work.

To every beautiful Black girl. Sis, I see you.

Contents

Introduction

Five months before the first draft of *Black Girl in Love (with Herself)* was due to the publisher, I found myself broken, a hot mess, and I barely recognized my life. How did I get here? This couldn't possibly be my picture-perfect life. This couldn't be the "good life" that I had spent the last four years carefully curating and creating and, of course, posting all over social media. The life that people commented on as if I were living the fairy tale. The life that people hashtagged #couplegoals.

My partner and I were the power couple. I was an acclaimed, award-winning writer, who turned her immigrant rags to riches story into a TV show. I was the first Black woman in Canada to have her own TV show (they called me the "Oprah" of Canada), and I now motivated thousands of women to take action on topics such as love, relationships, and just living their best damn lives! I loved my life and my work, and I truly thought I was doing God's work.

We often talked about our plans to leave a legacy, and with her brains, my creativity, and our strong work ethics, we knew we would change the world. I thought we were unstoppable! In our spare time we jet setted across the world. It was not unusual to catch us jumping on a plane to Dubai, England, Antigua, Barbados, or Hawaii. We ate at five-star restaurants around the world, taking pictures of our fabulous meals. We hired a car service to take us to the spa for the day. I often came home to five dozen roses on the counter, and, of course, I would Instagram that shit immediately! We often sent long, lovey dovey, public Facebook messages to each other, just to ensure that the world knew that we were in love. We were _that_ Black couple who had made it! We gave hope to all Black women that one day, they, too, could be living the fairy tale. I felt blessed that someone successful, rich, and gorgeous had chosen me, and I would pinch myself at night thinking, *How was this possible?* My relationship gave me a sense of identity and purpose. And if I'm being honest, it also gave me a sense of importance.

I was raised by a single mother who had me at age 17, and I spent most of my childhood being shuffled from one home to another. I grew up working class, in public housing, and got kicked out of the house at age 19. Yet somehow, I seemed to have achieved the impossible, and I was eager to share my secrets with the world. Here I was, the Black girl love expert who was going to tell how I had attracted the love of my life. I had done the work—inner and outer. I had spent the money on therapy. I had written *the list* where I told the Universe/God what I wanted in a partner, and I was not going to settle for less. I read that list every day until it was practically burned into in my brain. I had prayed the Ciara prayer, watched every episode of *Super Soul Sunday*, and by doing all of this, I had attracted my big love! I was the living example of never giving up hope. And love could find you too, girl! I knew so much about love that the biggest self-help publisher in North America gave me a damn book deal to write about it! Now suddenly, here I was in the fetal position—sleep deprived, crumpled on the bathroom floor, crying hysterically, gasping for air.

What the hell happened to my life?

Nothing made sense anymore. My fiancée of four years had just abruptly ended our relationship via text. Yes, girl, *text*! I was in disbelief. We were supposed to be getting married in Hawaii. And four weeks prior, we had moved into a brand-new luxury condo. Boxes were still unpacked, and we had recently hired a fancy interior decorator to create our beautiful home. I even had a date circled in my calendar to discuss paint colors for the nursery. Nursery? Oh, yes! I read that text while trying to wipe baby poop out of my shoulder-length locs. I had a brand-new, adopted baby boy who was just 12 days old and now I found myself with less than 10 days to vacate the apartment. The walls of my "perfect" life were crumbling. I was numb. The baby, picking up on my obvious stress, began screaming uncontrollably. I could not find the energy to go to him.

What the hell did I miss? How could I not know my relationship was in jeopardy? How could I have continued to offer thousands of women relationship advice and miss the tsunami hitting my own life? My inner critic, who I dubbed "Critical Cathy," quickly showed up to kick me while I was down. And, girl, she wasn't playing as her voice took over my head. *"Trey, you're an awful human being. And an awful mother. Everyone is going to laugh at you (full Carrie moment, minus the blood). This is all your fault! Why did you think someone like you could live a fairy-tale life? Haha! And now you've been dumped. You obviously don't have a clue what it takes to be in a relationship because if you did, your fiancée would still be here with you, making a bottle of formula. And if that weren't enough, now you and your baby are going to be homeless!"*

My life was in shambles, and the irony wasn't lost on me that I was supposed to turn in a book telling Black women how to live their best lives. "You're a fraud," Critical Cathy kept telling me over and over. How did I get here? I didn't have a damn clue. But I knew in order to figure this out, I had to dig deep to find the courage to accept that this moment, this very moment, was indeed my life. My sad, pathetic life. That I could not change. As painful as this moment was, this is where I was . . .

So, on the bathroom floor, I made a silent plea to the Universe: *Please show me the way. I don't want to die, but I don't want to live like this either.* I begged the Universe to show me the lesson in this. I broke down, weeping, my wails matching my baby's. And suddenly the baby stopped crying, and it was as if my entire world had stopped spinning. I heard a whisper, a soft voice from within, that said, *"Tell the truth. Tell the ugly truth. Tell all of it. Talk di tings! Your mess will be your message. And it will free others to live their truth . . ."*

A calmness came over me. I knew the Universe wasn't done with me yet. I had experienced a lesson that wasn't just for me alone. A divine assignment that I needed to share with others. A lesson on what to do with your life when it doesn't match up to the curated version that you have displayed on Instagram. On what to do when you are not chosen. What to do when you forgot how to love yourself because you were counting on someone else to love you. What to do when you didn't even know how to love yourself in the first place. Finally, I needed to share with Black women how to get back up from being a crumpled mess on the bathroom floor. Because sometimes, girl, you've got to get up and write a new chapter. A chapter that you were not expecting because you thought you had finished the damn book!

Slowly and painfully, I rose from the bathroom floor. It was 4:50 A.M., and the baby was due for his 5:00 A.M. bottle. I had to pull it together. I took a long, hard look in the mirror and saw a Black girl staring back at me with tears streaming down her face and snot running from her nose. I looked at her and said, "Hey, Trey, we are going to love you a little bit better, starting today. Starting right now, you're going to be a Black girl in love (with herself)."

chapter 1

Dear Mama

BLACK GIRL PLAYLIST:
"DEAR MAMA,"
TUPAC SHAKUR

My constant antics to impress my Jamaican, West Indian mother are often met with a raised eyebrow, a look of confusion, and her expressing the desire that I should have gone to med school or law school instead of "Prancing around on stage!" My mother has no clue how I ended up being a popular relationship/lifestyle coach. But often, from the stage, I will see her in the front row, trying to conceal a bashful, proud smile as she politely claps along with the packed audience filled with Brown and Black faces. She's the first to jump to her feet at every one of my talks as she looks around to ensure that everyone is giving me a standing ovation. Yet, she still can't hide her astonishment that I can fill a huge theater and that women pay to hear me speak. And no matter how many times I try to explain to her that I'm a professional motivational speaker, she still doesn't understand why corporations and organizations pay me lots of money to deliver keynotes about self-care, self-love, and putting yourself first.

"Trey, you're a wellness expert? What is all this nonsense?" My mother tries her best not to giggle, because everyone knows that I'm the "sensitive one" in the family, but I know she finds my profession quite comical and somewhat absurd. After all, she's a woman who worked three jobs in order to provide for her three children. In her world, there was no time for meditation, journaling, yoga, going to workshops to find your inner child, or holding hands and singing. To her, these are things that white people do, not us! Black women have no time for such nonsense!

So I was shocked when a few days after my bathroom breakdown, my mother came to see me, having driven from Tampa to Atlanta. Before her arrival, she never voiced her concern to me, but I could tell by the frequency of her FaceTime calls that she was worried. And I knew that she must be extremely worried to show up unexpectedly at my front door with my baby sister. Instead of asking how I was, she did what she did best. She headed to the kitchen to make all my favorite dishes—stewed peas and rice with pigtail and beef, and curried chicken and white rice. She heaped them on large plates and silently watched me eat. She also rearranged my kitchen, cleaned my entire home, and dutifully bathed, fed, cradled, and watched her new grandson while she shooed me away, telling me to get some sleep.

I must have looked like a wreck if my mother was encouraging me to sleep! My Jamaican mother viewed sleeping and laziness as the same thing. When I was growing up, my mother's favorite thing to do was to burst through our bedroom door at 7 A.M., yelling, "Okay, children, there must be something more constructive you could be doing with your time!" My mother would wake us for no apparent reason other than she was up, so everyone in the household needed to be up too! And now, here she was encouraging me to sleep. This had never happened in my lifetime.

My mother watched my slumped shoulders and water-filled eyes with caution. And through my closed bedroom door, I heard her and my sister whispering about my mental well-being. They were concerned. My mother assured my sister that I was a "fighter" and that I would get through this. After all, so many women in my family had been let down by love and life before and got back up. That's what all the women in my family did: We made it through. We didn't crumble, we didn't grieve. We just got up and kept going. No matter how much pain we were in, we didn't show it.

I knew this was what was expected of me, so I forced myself to put on a brave face for my family, biting down hard on my quivering lip every time I felt tears were going to fall. My mother wouldn't know what to do with an outpouring of my emotions. The women in my family were not emotional; we were brave, strong, and proactive. We were not women who fell apart because someone had hurt us or let us down. I tried to recall a time when I had seen my mother cry, but I couldn't. She didn't even cry at her own mother's funeral.

My mother is one of the bravest women I know. She is my superhero. My mother spent most of my childhood in full-out survival mode. She was born in Jamaica and came to England when she was 12 years old. At age 17, she had me, and a few years later, my brother was born, and several years later in her thirties she had my sister. In her early twenties she decided she wanted more and took the bold step of packing up her shit and moving to Canada, which beckoned as the land of opportunity. I was eight years old when my mother left me and my brother with our grandmother and moved to Canada. We were separated from our mother for four years. But eventually she was able to send for us. She had managed somehow to find an apartment in a working-class neighborhood and took pride in the fact that she had a shiny, brand-new silver Hyundai, which we piled into when she picked us up from the airport. My earliest memories of her consist of a tired-looking woman who was always rushing out the door, heading to her numerous jobs to provide for her family. As she left, she would rattle off a list of what needed to be done in her absence.

As the oldest, I was second-in-command, and she expected her 12-year-old daughter to step up. Laundry needed to be taken to the laundromat, the chicken needed to be taken out of the freezer. I needed to get the oven sprayed and clean the stove, give my brother dinner, help him with his homework, wash the dishes, season the chicken, and make our school lunches for the next day. My mother was the queen of multitasking and her favorite saying was "Learn to whistle and ride." Basically, she didn't think it was impossible to clean the stove while having a load of laundry in the dryer and quickly make bologna sandwiches at the same time. Each minute needed to be used efficiently. There was no time for sleep, and definitely no time for rest. Shit needed to get done! We knew that if we were not busy, we needed to act busy because my mother would find us something to do. And my mother had no time for wallowing in self-pity. Productivity was key in our household, and even if you were tired, worn out, hurt, scared, or overwhelmed, you just got back up and did what needed to be done. There was a big expectation placed on me to ensure that things got done.

So it was no surprise that this large-and-in-charge 12-year-old, who was her mother's right-hand girl, grew up to be an overachieving adult. I became the first Black woman in Canada to have a show, 'Da Kink in My Hair, on a prime-time TV network. It was a half-hour comedy based on my successful play of the same name. This little girl from the hood was now a big deal, but I felt like at any time, someone was waiting to snatch away all my success. That someone was monitoring me and waiting for me to mess up so they could take everything from me. I was suffering from a major case of impostor syndrome.

Sheryl Sandberg, in her book Lean In talks about this. She writes that every time she succeeded at something, she believed she had "fooled everyone yet again." And that "one day soon, the jig would be up." I think women of color, and especially Black women, face another loaded, layered version of this. Michelle Obama often talks about how women of color feel they have no right to be at the "success table"—even after they've achieved success. Because the higher we go up the ladder of success, the fewer and fewer faces we see that look like us. So we start to think perhaps it was a "mistake" or a fluke that we actually made it. Often, you may feel that you are indeed an impostor in your own life and that someone is going to discover you shouldn't be here.

I was experiencing extreme impostor syndrome and the anxiety of being "found out" was keeping me up at night. I wanted to prove to the world that I was the horse that you bet on. I prided myself on being a member of

"Team No Sleep," boasting that I only needed a mere four hours of rest per night to get through the day. I worked long hours and put ridiculous demands on my schedule. I loved long to-do lists and set up daily personal challenges to complete them. I'd wake up at 3 A.M., be on set at 4 A.M., and spend 12 hours per day reading, writing scripts, then acting in the show. After I wrapped filming, I'd invite myself into the editing suite to give my unsolicited advice on edits and cuts for the show—micromanaging and ensuring that everything was getting done the way I thought it should. Then I'd head over to the new wellness center I had just opened to give a talk or class or do some more micromanaging to make sure everything was running smoothly over there. Finally, I'd head home and deal with the medical care and needs of my terminally ill grandmother, who lived with me while she battled stage 4 cancer. After spending time with Granny and making sure she was okay, I'd go to my home office to brainstorm some more ideas for the show, watch the edits, and memorize my lines.

Some nights, I was so exhausted I fell asleep at my desk. Other times I'd get to bed just a few minutes before midnight and toss and turn for three hours before jumping out of bed to do it all over again. I was running on empty, and I ignored the telltale signs that all was not well with my body, such as my lack of sleep and occasional chest pain. And then one day, the shit hit the fan. I was in the editing suite when a sharp pain gripped my chest. I ignored it. And then it struck again. My body writhed in pain, and my left side felt numb. What did I do? Instead of telling anyone I was in pain, I asked for some tea. But then the pain became so unbearable that I actually keeled over onto the desk, alarming the editor and two producers in the suite. I finally confessed that for the last 20 minutes, I had been experiencing sharp chest pains. They tried to convince me to go to the hospital. Despite my assurances that I was fine—maybe it was the small beads of sweat on my forehead or the agony written across my face—they called an ambulance, and I was whisked away. All the while, I kept insisting that I was "fine."

"I'm fine." The Black woman's code for "There's really too much on my plate, but I'm going to try to figure it out all by myself. However, in the meantime, feel free to dump some more on my overflowing plate. And if some of the shit you dump on my plate falls on the floor, don't worry, I'll sweep it up. 'Cause I got this!"

We have witnessed generations of Black grandmothers, mothers, aunties, and sisters loudly declare, "I'm fine" while working two or three jobs where they are probably dealing with racism and sexism and often feel unseen and unheard, with little to no support in their homes or their workplace. They feel that they are weak for asking for help and try to carry the weight of the world on their shoulders, grinning all the while. They don't complain; they just take a deep breath and put on their superwoman cape as they fly off, yelling, "I'm fine!"

So now I'm in the emergency room, hooked up to a heart monitor. I was still on my BlackBerry, responding to e-mail, until a stern doctor barked at me to put it down. Didn't he know I was running an empire? I wanted to tell him, but something in his eyes told me this was serious. "Am I having a heart attack?" I asked.

"Are you concerned about your health?" the doctor asked.

This had to be a trick question. So I hesitated before slowly nodding yes.

He told me, "You are lucky that you did not have a heart attack, but you're close. Young lady, your heart rate is dangerously elevated. There is severe stress on your heart. Are you taking care of yourself?"

This one simple question, "Are you taking care of yourself?" reduced me to a blubbering mess. Care? Me? I should be taking care of myself? I began crying—the ugly, *Oprah*, snot-dripping-down-my-face cry. I didn't want to admit how tired and run-down I was. I didn't want to talk about the sleepless nights and my unhappiness. As my grandmother used to say, "My tired was tired!" I was supposed to be at the pinnacle of my success, yet I was miserable. I hated my life. I begged the doctor to admit me to the hospital for a few days—a week would be ideal! If I were in the hospital, I would finally have permission to take a much-needed rest without any judgment from my family, colleagues, and friends. No one would think that I was lazy or a quitter. If they said anything, I could feign outrage. "Can you believe it? Yes, I'm on bed rest! Strict orders from the doctor . . ."

The doctor looked at me in disbelief. "You want me to admit you so you can take a rest?" I nodded. He obviously didn't understand my life. He had no idea of the tremendous pressure I was under to run a successful TV show, manage a wellness center, look after a sick family member, and try to be the "fixer" for all my friends' lives.

It was obvious that he couldn't comprehend the reality of a Black female superhero!

The doctor shook his head. "You need to go home and rest. Tell your family and your friends that you need their help—"

I shot him a dirty look. The doctor signed my release with strict orders to take a rest and slow down. I went back to my life, but I didn't slow down. Instead, I added more to my plate. I was determined to be a success. And hard work equals success. I was working on the dream, working on the fairy tale called my life. The girl from the hood who made it out, who now had a life that was beyond anyone's wildest dreams.

And now here I was again, seven years later. Rock bottom and unable to tell my family I needed help. But this time, instead of continuing the charade, I had my first full emotional breakdown in front of my mother. I fully blame her for it. She burst into my home office and glanced at the clock. She was annoyed that I was engrossed in sending out work e-mail with the baby strapped to my chest. It was 7:45 P.M., and she wondered why I had not put the baby in the bath or fed him. She firmly reminded me of how important it was to keep him on a schedule. "Trey, 7:30 P.M. is his bedtime. You need to do better." I felt the quiet rage rise in me, and I tried to bite my lip, but this time, I had to say something. With my voice barely a whisper, I stated, "I'm not doing well, Mom . . ."

My mother, pretending that she didn't hear me, didn't make eye contact and headed to the bathroom to busy herself with running the baby's bath. I handed the baby to my sister, who had entered the room. Then I followed my mother, desperately trying to get her to look at me. The tearful words tumbled out without any warning.

"Mom, I'm really not doing well. I don't think I can do this."

I sat on the edge of the bathtub as a wave of emotions overtook me. I needed for her to see this pain. I needed to be okay to release it. The tears seemed to explode from someplace buried within me. Giant tears ran down my face, and my mother couldn't ignore it any longer. Awkwardly, she came over to me to pat me on the shoulder, which is the closest my mother has ever come to physical tenderness with me, and I knew she was trying her best. She didn't look at me but instead focused on a spot above my eyes. I knew she didn't want to fully witness my tears or the pain in my eyes. This was already too much for her.

"Trey, you're going to be fine. You must remember whose child you are, remember your grandmother, remember me. . . . We had it way worse, and we never gave up. You can't let this break you . . ."

And yes, my mother's solemn pep talk gave me some comfort, but I also recognized at that moment that my mother was not comfortable with my vulnerability or my emotion. My mother knew how to teach me to be strong, but she didn't know how to teach me to feel all my feelings, express them, live with them, acknowledge them, and sit with them. My mother could be my cheering squad, my person who reminded me to keep my chin up, but she couldn't be my safe, soft spot. She could not be the place where I could fall apart. And right then, I needed to fall apart . . . But she would not allow it. She believed that it was unsafe for Black women to fall apart. That there was no room in our lives for vulnerability or fragility. I needed to find that safe space for myself in order to survive. A safe space where I could cry with abandonment. My mother looked at me and said, "Now, go get the baby, he needs to be bathed." I nodded, swallowing my tears. We bathed my son together in a loaded silence.

That night, I started to think about whether I was this type of safe space for other Black women in my life. How many times, when despondent friends came to me, did I turn into my mother, reminding them of their strength and leaving empowering messages on their voice mail? I sent them Angela Davis quotes, but I never ever said to any of my friends, "Hey, sis, you may need to cry about that." I was also guilty of telling my sisters, "Girl, you've got this!" But what if you don't got it? What if you're so damn hurt and confused that you don't have the mental capacity to get back up? If I wanted to fall apart, could my sistah friends witness that and be okay with that? And could I be okay with them seeing me fall completely apart?

And that's what I needed someone to say to me—that it was okay to feel wounded. It was okay at this very moment to fall apart not once, not twice, but as often as needed.

How could I grant myself and other women permission to fall apart and how could I be intentional about creating safe spaces for them and myself? I sat with these thoughts for days, and I couldn't let them go. In my many moments of pondering, I was reminded of a quote by Audre Lorde:

"We have to consciously study how to be tender with each other until it becomes a habit because what was native has been stolen from us, the love of Black women for each other."

Audre Lorde was right: I knew how to be strong, yet I did not know how to be tender. My mother and grand-mother had made me the woman that I was, and without their valuable advice, I would never have made it this far and had this amazing life and career. But in delivering their "Gyal, get up and stop feeling sorry for yuself!" mes-saging, they forgot to show me or offer me tenderness—therefore, I did not know how to offer that to myself. And if there was ever a time that I needed tenderness, love, and care, now was the moment. I was tired of being a strong Black woman. I wanted to study how to be tender with myself.

SIS, GET YOUR MIND RIGHT!

1. What does tenderness mean to you?

2. How do you show yourself tenderness? How do you show others?

3. Was your mother/primary caregiver tender with you?

4. How can you improve in offering tenderness and compassion to yourself?

affirmations

I AM SO GLAD TO BE RECEIVING KIND AND TENDER LOVE.

I WORK HARD SO I REST WHEN MY BODY TELLS ME IT IS TIRED.

I LOVE AND ACCEPT MYSELF.

chapter 2

The Strong Black Woman

BLACK GIRL PLAYLIST:
"LADIES FIRST,"
QUEEN LATIFAH

My mother and grandmother instilled in me many valuable life lessons, and I'm a product of their ambition and strong work ethic. I remember as a little girl being in my bed and glancing at the clock to see it was 11 P.M. I could hear the familiar clanking of the ironing board and knew what my grandmother was doing. I climbed out of bed and watched through her cracked-open bedroom door as she sprayed starch on her blue work shirt. To this day, every time I hear the term "blue-collar worker," I think about my grandmother ironing her shirt each night.

My grandmother was tired, but there was a determined look on her face as she pressed her shirt with pride, getting ready for her night shift. She swept the train at night for London British Transport, and she was proud of her government job. My grandmother caught me watching her and gave me a weary smile before telling me to go back to bed. I had school in the morning and needed to get my sleep because learning requires a rested head. "Little girl, go to bed. Dat brain of yours needs rest. Yu' need to do good in school so you won't have to work at night like your poor granny." I went back to bed but was unable to sleep because my eight-year-old brain knew this wasn't right. It wasn't fair that I got to rest when my grandmother was so tired. It wasn't right that my tired grandmother had to leave her house in the dark to go to work. Yet I also vowed to work hard to make my grandmother proud and so that maybe one day, she wouldn't have to work so hard.

Later in adulthood, whenever I felt the need to rest or complain, I would scold myself and say, "Your grandmother left her house every night to sweep a damn train, and you want to complain about your comfortable life? Stop being lazy and get it done!" At the height of my television success, I was well aware that in one month, I probably made more money than my grandmother made in a year. So, I didn't have the right to complain about anything. My mother and grandmother had it so much worse, so how dare I complain about life being hard?

If you gather a group of successful Black women, many of us will share tales of what our grandmothers and mothers sacrificed for us to have the success we have today. We wear our mothers' sacrifices as a badge of honor. This is exemplified in a quote attributed to Sydney Labat, a Black medical student who tweeted it along with an image of 15 Black medical students in their white lab coats standing outside of a slave quarters: "We are truly our ancestors' wildest dreams."

It was not uncommon for our mothers to do without in order to pay for our college tuition or work several jobs to pay for our books, housing, and food. We have seen them get up, worn and tired, to provide for us, and we were reminded every day how much they sacrificed for their children. From them we learned the unspoken rule: "You work hard, you don't complain, 'cause ain't no one got time for that!"

To mirror the strength and grit of our mothers and grandmothers, many of us continue to ignore our fatigue, burnout, and our bodies' stress signals. We ignore the fact that we are falling apart because the running dialogue in our head is, "Girl, get up and be strong! You can do it!"

Yet that night in the bathroom, as my life was falling apart and my mother was giving me her stern pep talk about survival, I knew I needed more. The strong Black woman trope was no longer working for me. I wasn't feeling strong. I was scared, overwhelmed, and petrified of my own perceived weakness. I knew I needed to create a safe space to fall apart.

FINDING YOUR SAFE SPACE

Trey, find your safe space. I wrote that in my journal, but as my life continued to tailspin, it fell to the bottom of my list. But the Universe has a way of reminding you of what you need.

It was 1:30 A.M., and I had been a new mother for less than two weeks. My mother and sister returned home, convinced that I had it all under control. How could I not? I was a fighter, not a quitter. But that night, the baby cried nonstop. All my efforts to figure out what was wrong weren't working. I paced back and forth, holding the screaming baby in my arms. How could I not calm him down? I felt like a failure. I began crying. *This is too much*, I thought, so I reached for my phone. I needed help. I attempted to call my friend, Trecia. *No, it's too late.* I hung up the phone before it started ringing. The baby was still screaming. Twenty minutes later, I knew I couldn't take a minute more. It was after 2:00 A.M. I quickly dialed Trecia's number again. Thankfully, she answered. I yelled into the phone. "I need help! I can't do this!" Fifteen minutes later, Trecia was at the door. She took one look at me—I was disheveled and panicked—and grabbed the crying baby.

"Girl, go to bed." I protested. She gave me a stern look that said, "I got this." I retreated to my bed and could hear Trecia soothing the crying baby. Guilt rushed over me as my weary head hit the pillow, and I slept for seven solid hours.

I knew Trecia was now one of my safe places. She assured me that she and her wife would be there for me. And they were. They made a care schedule for me, ensuring that for the next four weeks, I had someone who would be there at night with the baby. She and her wife assured me that I wasn't a lousy mother and that what I needed was support. They showed up time and time again without me asking. And if there is anything I learned in this process of falling apart, it is how important it is to have friends who allow you to come undone and who pick up all your broken pieces and patch you back together.

They allowed me to go over all the painful details of my breakup over and over again. They allowed me to cry. And yes, they sometimes offered me encouraging pep talks, but they also stood in the gap, bearing witness to my pain. They didn't look away.

CAN WHITE WOMEN BE OUR SAFE PLACES?

I have two very close white friends. Lisa is Jewish and has known me most of my adult life. She has gone through every single heartbreak with me, and I can honestly say she knows me better than anyone. Carys is my business and writing partner and, over the years, has become a dear friend. I have a rule about having white friends. If I cannot talk about race and you can't acknowledge that life is harder for me as a Black woman than it is for you, we can't be friends. If I can't call you and tell you "to go and get your people because they messed up again!" we can't be friends. If your response to #blacklivesmatter is #alllivesmatter, we can't be friends. So my white girlfriends are some of the dopest chicks I know. They are fierce feminists who are constantly checking their privilege, and we have deep, thoughtful discussions about race, sexism, and life. So during the period when my life was falling apart, I realized I was very different when around my two closest white friends. With them, I cried my eyes out. Each of them encouraged me to cry while also being very affectionate with me. The first time I saw Lisa, I rushed into her arms, and she cradled me like a baby and gave me the longest hug. She held me for at least five minutes while whispering into my ear that everything was going to be okay. I realized that I didn't have this level of physical intimacy with any of my Black sistah friends, and I was very curious. Why didn't I feel safe requesting or desiring physical comfort from them? And why did I feel a need to perform "I got this." Why was I scared to show my Black friends that I wasn't as STRONG as I had let them all believe? There was an unwritten Black girl code, of "Sis, get the fuck back up!" that I had unfortunately prescribed to. So when my Black friends reached in to hug me, I was uncomfortable with their tenderness and affection and would brush them off. I wanted them to know I wasn't "weak." So I constantly assured them that I was doing okay . . .but they all knew I was lying.

But when it came to Carys, I was comfortable with her affection. And I allowed her to comfort me. She's a towering brunette, close to 6 feet, and I'm barely 5 feet. Upon seeing me, she scooped me up in her arms while tenderly stroking mine as I practically cried into her belly button! A few days into her visit, she sat me down and firmly said, "Trey, I don't think you're crying enough about this. You need to cry and let it out. Stop being strong . . ."

And she was right. I needed to stop acting strong. I needed to let ALL my friends know that I wasn't doing well. I was a big emotional mess. Barely holding it together. My heart felt as if it had been scattered across the floor of my apartment and I was desperately trying to find all the pieces. I barely recognized the girl looking back at me. My thoughts were a jumbled mess. And every day I vowed that today would be the day I would pull myself together. I was so used to being strong that I had actually given myself a deadline for when this grief needed to be over. I had forbidden myself to cry anymore. But I just couldn't stop. And what I soon realized is grief doesn't have a timeline. I didn't need to get back on the horse, I needed to throw myself on the ground and wail. I needed to sit in this pain and feel every single ounce of it to survive and learn the lessons.

I was thankful for friends who showed up in droves to hold me, listen to me, hold the baby, pack boxes, bring food, check in on me. I was proud that I had cultivated a circle who were determined to show up for me in my time of need, because that wasn't always the case. As I've gotten older, I have become more selective with my friendships. I now know that I need friends who will give me pep talks. I need friends who will physically hold me. I need friends who will give me the harsh, plain truth, and I need friends who will just sit with me in the grief.

SIS, GET YOUR MIND RIGHT!

1. Do you have a friend with whom you would feel safe having a full meltdown?

2. What does cultivating a safe space mean to you?

3. When comforting a friend, are you physically intimate with them? If not, why?

4. Have a discussion with your sistah circle about physical intimacy in your friendship. What could it look like or be?

affirmations

I AM BEAUTIFUL, SUCCESSFUL, AND CONFIDENT.

I LISTEN TO MY BODY, AND I REST WHEN NEEDED.

TENDERNESS TO MYSELF IS MY BIRTHRIGHT,
AND I PRACTICE IT EVERY DAY.

I AM GLAD THAT I AM LOVED AND
SUPPORTED WHEREVER I GO.

chapter 3

Sis, Who's Got Your Back?

BLACK GIRL PLAYLIST:
"FRIENDS,"
JODY WATLEY

"Everyone wants to ride with you in the limo, but what you want is someone who will take the bus with you when the limo breaks down."

—OPRAH WINFREY

If you're an old-school head like me, you will remember this one! Jody Watley telling us to question if we indeed have real friends. At the heart of the song was the question, "Do you have friends that you can count on?"

I used to blast this from my boombox and rewind that cassette at least a hundred times. Do you remember cassette tapes and how, sometimes, you had to use a pencil to fix it when the tape got messed up? But I digress. Let's get back to friendships. My fourth-grade teacher, Miss Shepps, expressed to my grandmother in a parent-teacher meeting, "Trey has the amazing ability to lead all her friends. They all do what she says, and she is a leader. But I worry that she spends way too much of her time organizing her friends' lives and bossing them around instead of worrying about her own. She needs to understand that the concept of friendship is a give and take; she cannot always be the leader. She needs to let friends help her sometimes."

Unfortunately, my grandmother and I took no notice of Miss Shepps. My grandmother quickly rushed me out of the room. Once we were out of earshot, she whispered, "Dat white lady don't know nothing! Trey always be a leader, not a follower! Don't count on anyone but yourself! Never need anyone more than they need you!"

I nodded. Granny was right. We both knew Miss Shepps was wrong. Very wrong!

Plus, I never liked Miss Shepps, and Granny was convinced that she was trying to instill in me "foolish North American ways" that were in direct opposition to my grandmother's belief that you didn't need a circle of support, especially when you had assigned yourself as the leader.

Yet, I now realize I should have taken heed of some of Miss Shepps's advice, especially when years later, nothing much had changed. I went from being an eight-year-old bossy best friend to being a thirtysomething bossy best friend. I prided myself on my ability to rearrange all my friends' lives. I took great joy in being the go-to person who everyone called when they were having problems with their man, momma, boss, or kids! You name it, "Trey would fix it!"

It took me many years to figure out that I could actually get paid to help people with their lives and that this was a skill to be valued! I've always had an amazing instinctual ability to be able to figure out what people needed, and I was able to break down complicated problems in minutes and offer invaluable solutions. I loved being able to provide clear plans of actions for my stressed-out friends. I would spend hours on the phone, consoling them, doling out sage advice, and gleefully sharing life tips that I had read in self-help books or watched on *Oprah* or *Dr. Phil*. I was everyone's spiritual advisor, counselor, coach, and the person to whom they confessed all their deepest sorrows and secrets. Friends knew they could call me at any hour of the day, and I was always there in every crisis.

To be honest, I secretly enjoyed being the responsible one, the level-headed one, and the problem solver. I reveled in my role of being the person who others referred to as their godsend, their most trusted advisor. My grandmother would often compliment me and say, "That girl has her head on her shoulders." Or she would proudly declare that I was the only one in the family who had common sense. Yet, because I portrayed myself as the person who had it all together, I rarely, if ever, went to my friends for support or advice. I frequently problem-solved alone, cried alone, and kept all my issues to myself. None of my friends had ever seen me cry, which I wore as a badge of honor. Yet at my house, I managed to have a steady supply of Kleenex for all my needy friends. And although I had a huge circle of people whom I referred to as my BFFs or sisters, I felt terribly lonely. I didn't trust that any of them would actually support me in a crisis. I felt drained, unsupported, and overwhelmed in trying to balance everyone else's lives plus my own!

The true state of my friendships didn't become clear to me until after a tearful session with my therapist, where I shared that I was moving. I was shutting down my office and had spent the entire week packing boxes in my old house to unpack in my new house, plus I was handling the health care of my grandmother while also producing shows. I was drained, tired, overwhelmed, and I shamefully admitted defeat. My solution was to hire some movers or a packing service to help me pack. My therapist asked, "Why do you need to pay people to help you? Have you asked any of your friends to help you?"

I was shocked the thought hadn't entered my mind. I did not know how to ask for help, and to be honest, I wasn't even sure that if I asked any of my friends that they would show up, which saddened me. I didn't trust that I had a circle of friends who would support me enough to even come by and pack a box. My therapist encouraged me to list 10 of my closest friends and send an e-mail to them asking for help. She told me to suggest three reasonable time slots for them to come and help me for two hours. I was scared shitless! I never asked for help and didn't even know where to begin. I also knew that by sending this e-mail, it would also reveal to me what I knew deep down: I really didn't have friends that I could count on. I basically had three types of friends. Some of them may seem familiar to you.

THE CAMERA-READY GOOD-TIME FRIEND

Camera-ready good-time friends are only there when the good times are happening. They were the ones who would show up whenever I had a flashy opening party, was offering them free tickets for a screening, or was throwing some sort of party and had space in the limo. They would only call to find out what was going on, and before agreeing to go anywhere with me, they would ask who would be in attendance to ensure it was worth their time and effort.

And then they would show up in a new outfit. In fact, camera-ready good-time friends usually begin each conversation by telling you how much they just spent on a new outfit, or what they just read on the latest fashion blog. And they spend a lot of time jet-setting, partying, and going to red carpet events. They have developed an art to name-dropping and often call everyone darling or say everything is fabulous! They also tend to air-kiss both cheeks. I always felt with my camera-ready good-time friends that they were more invested in how far I could assist them with climbing the social ladder than actually trying to create a deep friendship with me. I knew that my camera-ready good-time friends would not be interested in helping me pack my kitchen in their designer outfits!

THE BAG-OF-BAD-NEWS FRIEND

Bag-of-bad-news friends carry around an invisible sack, similar to the one Santa hauls around. Yet inside are beautifully wrapped gifts of depression and bad news! It's not unusual in the space of one week for their husbands to leave them, their cat to die, and for them to get hit by a bus! Anytime you have any sort of good news, they usually reply with, "Must be nice . . ." These are the friends who regularly dump on you. They tell you everything that has gone wrong in their life starting from when they were in their mother's womb! They start each sentence with a loud, heavy sigh. They are known to burst into tears often. They have major problems with their mother, partners, kids, and co-workers. Basically, everyone really. They hate life, and they hate themselves. They are often going through a breakup or some sort of emotional stress.

Bag-of-bad-news friends never ask about me, and most of their conversations are spent carefully dissecting all the bad things that have happened to them. Bag-of-bad-news friends usually don't need a response as much as they need an audience. You could put the phone down while they are talking, return 15 minutes later, and they would not even have noticed you were gone. They show up at your house unannounced, eyes red and nose runny, at all hours of the night, to just "vent." They often get jealous of any new friends you may have, and often feel "left out" if you express that you are going somewhere without them or God forbid actually try to live a happy life! They are such big babies that sometimes it feels like the only thing you can do is pull your titty out and put it in their mouths to console them!

THE DRAMA DIANA FRIEND

These friends call at all hours of the day and expect you to drop everything to help them. They leave frantic voice messages such as, "Call me, it's an E-M-E-R-G-E-N-C-Y!" They are always in some sort of crisis, and always have some sort of big conflict or high drama they are going through. Usually, it involves matters of the hearts or family drama: an affair with a married man, they've missed their period and aren't sure who the father is, they just got kicked out of their house, they need to borrow $500 to pay their rent because they are minutes away from being evicted!

Drama Diana friends are born actors and thrive on delivering play-by-play re-enactments of their "final" ultimatum conversation with their married boyfriend. They often enlist your help to break into their boyfriend's voice mail, drive by their ex's house, or help stalk a bitchy co-worker's Facebook page. They often ask you to decode random text or e-mail messages from their ex, husband, sister, or mother. Often you feel as if you are having the same conversation with them over and over, and they seem to be having the exact same conflict with different people. They take no accountability for their actions and swear up and down that this time things are going to be different. After a phone call with Drama Dianas, you feel drained and have a sinking feeling in your stomach that you will hear from them again in about five minutes for help to put out another bush fire! I knew my Drama Diana friends would not have time to help me pack a box; they were too busy arguing with their boyfriend's wife!

SIS, GET YOUR MIND RIGHT!

Get out your journal. It's time to do some deep soul searching and examine your closest friendships. Find a quiet place where you won't be interrupted, then ponder the following prompts:

1. Gut response: How do you feel when you see your closest friend's phone number come up on your call display? Is your first response to let the call go to voice mail? Or do you eagerly rush to the phone, dying to share your day and events? How do you feel after a conversation with your friend? Do you feel happy? Inspired? Relaxed? Or do you feel emotionally drained? Bored? Annoyed?

2. Give and take: What percentage represents how much you think you give to this friendship? 50 percent? 70 percent? No friendship or relationship is balanced all the time; however, the percentages should switch back and forth. You should never be the one who is always giving more of the emotional support while getting little in return. Is your friend always taking from you and not filling up your emotional piggy bank? Also, when you are in need, is she the person you think of calling to share good news and bad?

3. Growth. Does this friendship help you grow? If you met your friend today at an intimate dinner party, would you be eager to sit next to her? Would you be intrigued by her? Would you want to invite her to your home to meet your significant other or your kids? Would she still be someone you want to be friends with? Would her conversation inspire you? Would her belief system complement yours? Would her drive and dreams inspire you? Would you share the same interests? Would you have enough in common?

4. Would this friend "hold the baby"? Would this friend be the person you call in your darkest hour? Would this friend be able to hold you and your grief? Would she drop everything and show up at 2 A.M. so you could:

A. Cry
B. Rant
C. Sleep
D. Bury the body! (Just kidding!)

Sis, we all need a friend who we know has our back at all costs. In my darkest hours, I have friends who will sit on the phone with me for hours and hours. I have a friend who flew in from Los Angeles to Atlanta for 24 hours just so I could cry and rant. Another friend flew from Wales to Tampa to help me look after the baby. She knew I was feeling overwhelmed, and most of the time, she simply listened as I cried and blew my nose on her sweater. Sis, you need friends like that.

After completing this exercise, take a few days to think about what you wrote before you take any action. If your current friendships do not add value to your life, you may need to let them go.

affirmations

I'M SO HAPPY TO HAVE AMAZING FRIENDS
WHO LOVE AND SUPPORT ME.

EVERYWHERE I GO, I AM LOVED AND CELEBRATED.

I LOVE EVERYONE, AND THAT LOVE IS
MIRRORED BACK TO ME AT ALL TIMES.

chapter 9

I Know We're Family, but You're a Hot Mess!

"Wherever we lived, we were often the only black family, and certainly the only Haitian family. But my parents were really great at providing a loving home where we could feel safe and secure."

—ROXANE GAY

Have you been to a family Thanksgiving dinner where the creepy uncle is in attendance? The uncle that everyone knows has acted inappropriately with many of the young girls in the family. In hushed tones, we are warned not to be alone with him or to keep an eye on him. Yet, there he is at the dinner table at every damn family gathering! And then there's the aunt who is going to explode at the dining table right after the turkey is sliced because she's on her sixth drink? She's the one who probably will tell creepy uncle to "go fuck yourself!" She is carrying around years of pain and trauma. Yet everyone will just say she can't hold her liquor. And then there's the family member who shows up with dark glasses, trying to conceal her black eye, or the cousin who shows up with his "friend" and everyone knows he's gay, but no one talks about it.

For Black women, family is sometimes the most unsafe place. Many of us come from families with prevalent and fully operational cycles of trauma. Often, when you are the one who wishes to heal yourself or your family, you're viewed as the "troublemaker" or the "sensitive one" or trying to "act white." My favorite meme is, "I'm in therapy to deal with the people in my family who should be in therapy!" #nolietoldhere.

How true is that? Sis, sometimes, we need to create boundaries with our family to safeguard our mental well-being. While I was dealing with motherhood, my hellish breakup, and the shit show called my life, fate put my sister's plans for her dream wedding into motion. My little sister was marrying the man of her dreams, and love was definitely in the air—just not for me. My sister sent numerous group texts encouraging us to buy blush shoes to match our earrings and dresses, while I wanted to throw myself into oncoming traffic. But I was the maid of honor. I love my sister, and she's always supported me, and I wanted to return the favor. So, three weeks before her big event, I packed up Baby Bear, and we went to stay with her and help with the wedding. (Also, I now was officially homeless, and all my stuff was in storage while I tried to figure out what the hell to do with my life. So the timing was perfect to go to Tampa and help plan the wedding of the year.)

By day three of my stay, I realized my trip was a big mistake. My sister has a type A personality. She has her Ph.D. in math—that she got at age 27! Need I say more? She's about order, structure, and everything going according to plan. And her quest to have everything perfect for her big day was wreaking havoc on my own well-being. Her stress was adding to my stress, and the constant bickering between her and my mother was out of control. I felt as if the walls were caving in on me. Every interaction with my mother and my sister was draining. So I decided I needed to take a break. My mother and sister were perplexed about why I would need time alone and why I was bailing on them a week before the wedding. Also, my mother was concerned about how my absence would be perceived by family traveling in for the wedding. "How would that look?" she asked before answering her own question. "It would look disgraceful!" But I no longer had the need or desire to worry about keeping up appearances. I had to step away to continue with my own healing. I knew that to be a Black girl in love with myself, I needed to set some time and distance in place with my family. I packed up Baby Bear and drove six hours to the beach so I could clear my head. And yes, my family viewed this decision to take care of myself and be alone while they were planning the biggest event of our family's history as selfish and unsupportive, but I knew I needed to save myself. Giving my sister what she wanted from me was not possible. I could not be her emotional support when my gas tank was empty, and I was essentially running on fumes.

I explained that I could not participate fully in most of the wedding planning as it was too much at that time.

I planned to do some radical self-care while away. My friend Carys flew in from Wales to help me look after Baby Bear. She came armed with bottles of wine and ice cream. Instead of participating in wedding hell, I spent my days journaling, writing my book, walking along the beach, crying, going to the hot tub, getting massages, gobbling down ice cream, and drinking bottles and bottles of cheap wine! My family wasn't pleased, but they knew from past experiences that once I set a family boundary, I usually follow through.

Just ask my grandmother! She's dead now, but hey! My grandmother used to be a news junkie. She would stay glued to CNN, 24 hours per day. She watched no other programming unless it was *The Young and the Restless* at 4 P.M. Gran was the person who I would start and end my day with, and every morning at 7 A.M., she'd call me to "Just say good morning." Usually, before I could croak out, "Good morning," in response, she would give me a recap of the daily news, what country had been bombed, who had been killed, what state the economy was in, what foods you shouldn't eat because they would give you cancer, and a full recap of the Michael Jackson trial. And then at 10 P.M, she would call to ensure that I got in okay and again tell me more depressing news that she might have missed in our morning call.

After getting off the phone with her, I would often feel a sense of doom and some level of anxiety. But I got so used to our daily calls that I didn't even realize there was a direct connection to my anxiety and our conversations. It finally clicked one day when Granny was on one of her rants. I had this clear signal from the Universe in the form of a little voice that said, "Don't start your day with her because it won't be a good day!"

So, I stopped cold turkey. I decided that I would turn off the ringer on my phone, and I chose to consciously start my day peacefully. This included daily meditation, journaling, and reading or listening to something motivational. I love listening to motivational speakers such as Les Brown, Lisa Nichols, Eric Thomas, or Jack Canfield in the morning. Or listening to a motivational self-help book. I find that it's a great way to keep your mornings sacred and also ensure that you start your day with positive energy.

My grandmother wasn't too happy with all my changes. When she finally confronted me about why wasn't I taking her calls in the mornings, I wish I could say that I put on my big girl panties and was honest and said, "Hey, Gran, you're toxic and I can't damn well deal with you in the morning!" But I have a Jamaican granny and there are just somethings you can't get away with saying without the risk of losing your teeth. So instead I lied—yeah, I lied! I told my granny that I had enrolled in an early-morning exercise class at the gym. She was over the moon and so glad that her chubby granddaughter was finally working on her weight! I was glad that I had taken control of my morning routine, and I now began the day more relaxed and focused.

SIS, GET YOUR MIND RIGHT!

1. With whom in your family do you need to create some boundaries?

2. What would those boundaries look like? Limit contact? Have fewer phone calls? Don't make or allow personal visits? Don't start your day with that person?

3. Which family member do you enjoy spending time with? How can you spend more time with them? Are there any family members with whom you want to reconnect?

affirmations

MY FAMILY IS BLESSED AND HIGHLY FAVORED.

MY FAMILY LOVES AND SUPPORTS ME.

EVERYONE IN MY FAMILY, INCLUDING ME, IS THRIVING, GROWING, AND AT PEACE.

chapter 5

Mo' Money Mo' Problems

BLACK GIRL PLAYLIST:
"MO MONEY MO PROBLEMS,"
NOTORIOUS BIG

"The most important aspect of keeping your money is being aware of how much of it you are spending."

—TIFFANY ALICHE, THE BUDGETNISTA

Sis, I'm going to bet that if you have a copy of this book, you're probably what I playfully call the "first one rich." Because the "first one rich" is usually the one who turns to self-help books to try to figure out how to lead a more balanced life, how to improve herself, and how to be a better person overall . . . and also how to keep your family out of your pocket! Because maybe you're not rich rich! But you got some coin, and you're the person who's got a little notebook with the names of the family members who still owe you your damn money! You're probably viewed as the one who "made it." You are usually considered the "fancy auntie"—the one who is used as the family example of someone who's got her life together, and despite all the odds stacked against her, made lemonade out of lemons. You're the one friends and family call "lucky." The one who seems on paper to have it all together.

But what folks don't know is, it can be extremely lonely at the top. The late nights you are pulling at work leave little time for a relationship or limited time for your family and loved ones. You are constantly competing against yourself, trying to prove that you are indeed worthy of this success. You may or may not be living above your means, trying to fit the mold of what success looks like. And God knows it can be expensive trying to keep up appearances. Living in the right zip code, driving the right car, having the designer handbag, can all be financially exhausting, even for a type A personality who is used to juggling several balls in the air at once. And somehow, you're keeping that shit together because, after all, you're the go-to person for all your friends. The one they go to when they are running a bit short on their rent, or need someone to spot them a little cash because their car just broke down, or you're the person who can just "hold" them over until they get their next paycheck, or the one who needs to help momma with some grocery money . . . And of course, you are always the person who picks up the tab at every girl's night out. You make good money, so they all know that you can afford to have a nice home, a nice car, take fabulous vacations, and enjoy a nice glass of wine and a gourmet dinner at a five-star restaurant.

But while doing all those things, you feel guilty. Why? Because you're probably the most successful person in your family. You feel guilty that your older sister works really hard at her nine-to-five job, but you make more money than she does. You feel guilty that your momma has arthritis in her left knee that acts up when it rains, but she is still working, and while you can give her some money at the end of the month, you don't have enough money to tell her to quit her job. You feel guilty that your baby brother got into a little trouble when he was a teen and now, he can't find a job while it seems you are living high off the hog. You are living a life that they could only dream of. And because of this guilt, you feel a need to continue to look after grown-ass adults in your family! Yeah, I'm gonna tell some truth today, because, sis, this is what we're not going to do anymore!

A former client of mine came to see me in shock and disbelief. Her accountant had just done her taxes and had asked her about unknown expenses coming out of her account to the tune of $35,000! My client tearfully expressed that she didn't realize that loans or "can you spot me until Tuesday?" handouts to her brother and mother had added up to $35,000 in one year! Basically, she had her family on payroll. And many of us who are the success stories in our families do this all the time. We try not to keep track of how much money we are giving our families because if we did, it would make us rethink a lot of things in our lives. We don't realize several $500 loans can start adding up. Not to mention that many of us have jumped on as co-signers for mortgages and loans and now find ourselves left with the monthly payments because Little Poochie up and lost his job.

Recently, I was working with a client who was the first person in her family to ever attend college. She was a successful attorney, making six figures. When her grandmother got Alzheimer's, she moved her grandmother in. Her younger sister also moved in to "help" with her grandmother's care. But it was clear that the sister was actually looking for a place to stay and three square meals. She was adding to the financial burden of my client, who was now paying for a full-time nurse, her grandmother's expenses, and the additional expenses of her sister, who always was short on cash. When I suggested that she needed to give her sister a notice—i.e., tell her sister a specific time and date to get the hell outta of her house!—my client looked at me as if I was crazy. She was scared. She worried that it would look like she was throwing her freeloading sister out on the streets. What would her other family members think? How could she do this to her own sister? We wrote out an action plan and script of what she would say to her sister. It was a softer version of: "Get the hell out of my house." We changed it to "I think it's time you explore other options in housing." My client and I role-played this conversation so she could get comfortable with the script. We also rehearsed what she would say to any meddling family members who wanted to offer their opinions. It took nearly six months for my client to build up the courage to make some changes. And the fallout was swift. Other family members indeed had a lot to say! "What! You're throwing your poor sister out? How can you sleep at night?" Yet none of them offered to take her trifling ass in! Eventually, her sister found an apartment. My client offered to pay for the first four months of rent while her sister actively sought employment. My client stuck to her guns, and guess what? Baby sister eventually found a job, and she even went back to school. She started to take ownership of her life. What my client learned was that she could help her sister within reason, but she was not responsible for her sister's overall well-being. Being successful does not mean that you have to financially support everyone in your family.

I had a friend who owned several successful businesses. She's a self-made millionaire, and whenever we went out with friends, she would order several bottles of $700 wine. She would grab the bill every time it came to the table, which could easily be a couple thousand dollars. She never batted an eye at the amount and just whipped out her black credit card. Even when it was her birthday, she paid for everyone, no matter how much we insisted otherwise. She also paid for lavish holidays for her friends and family. Uncomfortable with the financial dynamic being played out in our friendship, I sat her down for a heart to heart. As a relationship and lifestyle coach, I knew there was more going on. She wasn't just generous, and there was some emotional unpacking that needed to happen. After some gentle prodding, she eventually admitted that she felt that "buying" people was her way to feel loved. She didn't feel people could possibly love her just for her. We traced this back to her childhood. She had a tumultuous relationship with her mother, and her brother, who was two years younger than her, was her mother's favorite. Her mother would always tell her that she would never amount to anything. So to prove her mother wrong, she became a successful entrepreneur. She was always trying to please her mother, and no matter what she did, her mother never told her she loved her or was proud of her. Each one of her friends represented the unrequited love of her mother. She thought that if she was overly generous to her friends, they would give her the love that her mother couldn't. I strongly encouraged my friend to go to therapy to deal with the rejection of her mother and to explore how this played out in her everyday relationships with other women.

TRACING YOUR HERSTORY ABOUT MONEY

For many years, money was my biggest block. I used to say that I wasn't good with money, and this would be my daily mantra. And, of course, if you keep saying something, eventually, it becomes your core belief and will show up in your life to show just how true it is. I had grown up in a household where, often, there was never enough money. I have vivid memories of my mother being stressed about money, debating what bill to pay and what could possibly wait until the next week. I would overhear arguments between her and my stepfather about money. Often, my mother would express fears about losing our house. So I promised myself that I would one day take care of my mother, so she didn't have to worry about finances. I knew I needed to do something different with my life if I didn't want to have the same financial issues as my mother. Yet, I didn't know any wealthy Black person. I had no money mentors. In high school, my family moved from Toronto Community Housing (a housing project) to a middle-class neighborhood outside of the city. My mother was determined to give her family a fighting chance and opportunities she didn't have. She wanted us to go to a good school and live the dream that was costing her everything to provide. Financially strapped, my mother was tired, frustrated, and desperately trying to hold it all together. Even though she was proud to own a home, she never enjoyed it. None of us did. The bitter arguments about money persisted with her and my stepfather, and the threat of them losing the house poisoned any joy of homeownership.

This kept me up at night. Where would we go? I was scared that we would be homeless, and this fear stayed with me throughout my entire life.

I started working part time to help with the household bills and to also have some extra cash. I also wanted to keep up with the extravagant lifestyle of my peers. It was the first time that I was around children whose families had generational wealth and vastly more money than mine. Many of my classmates came from families who had thriving family businesses, and their parents had been stacking away money for their first car, college education, first home, and wedding, while my mother was struggling to just get by with no additional resources to think long term. Yet, many of my peers' families often sat down with their children to discuss their financial future. They were having conversations about wealth that my family was incapable of having. After school, when my classmates would head to the mall to go shopping, I would join them, but not to shop. It was to go to meet my grandmother, who had a job at the mall's food court wiping tables. I would often go and keep my grandmother company or help the other elderly women of color who were working there. They welcomed me, proud to see me in my school uniform, and they beamed when my grandmother shared with them that I was now school president. They gave me valuable words of wisdom and told me to work hard so one day my grandmother wouldn't have to work so hard. I assured them that I would. I had dreams to not only retire my grandmother but thought of how great it would be to have enough money to tell all of the elderly "aunties" who worked in the mall to stop working "because I got you!"

I didn't have the language to be able to name that what I was experiencing with my classmates was a class imbalance. Instead, I hoped that no one would notice that the lack of money was a constant worry for me. I tried my best to be witty, smart, outgoing, and funny and made fun of myself before anyone else did. So I was well-liked and popular, but secretly, I carried around this money insecurity.

In high school, I met a lifetime friend who truly changed the trajectory of my life—Raquel. She was Jamaican. Her father was a former judge in Jamaica, and her family owned their own law firm. She lived in Stonegate, the most affluent neighborhood in the city. The first time she invited me to her home, I was blown away. It was huge. The house was pristine. Her mother was an avid art collector, and expensive art by Black artists hung on pristine white walls. In one of their many rooms, they had a baby grand piano, and in their kitchen was a joyful housekeeper. A Black family with a damn housekeeper! I tried to hide my amazement. Raquel's parents drove matching Mercedes-Benzes and often attended art openings and the theater. They were rich rich! I knew this because when Raquel's running shoes were dirty, she didn't throw them in the washing machine—or scrub them with a toothbrush, soak the laces in bleach, and leave them on the steps to dry like I did. She just threw them away, and her mother bought her a brand-new pair! Often, Raquel's mother would be painting beautiful watercolors in her sunroom that overlooked a lush backyard, while easy jazz played in the background. Unlike my mother, she seemed to not have a worry in the world. They were living the real-life Cosby Show on steroids. I now knew that it was possible to be rich and Black, and I vowed to be like them.

Yet later, even when I began to make six figures-plus, I always felt there was never enough money and that one day I would run out of it. And the additional zeroes at the end of my bank account statement did not help soothe my fears. I worried about becoming the female version of MC Hammer, who had all this money and one day woke up broke. Making more money became my ultimate goal, and trying to enjoy it left me conflicted. So I was living way below my means because I didn't want to end up on the streets.

When I got my own TV show and my first check, I thought accounting must have made a mistake, so I ran to the bank to cash it before they found out. True story. I was shocked I could make this much money. Lucky for me, it wasn't a mistake, and I soon realized that some serious money can be made from writing, acting, and producing your own show. With my weekly paycheck, I was surely making more money than any of my family and friends. And although I tried to help them as much as I could financially, even hiring several of my family members and friends to work on the show, I still felt a tremendous sense of guilt. Guilt about making money from something as "frivolous" as acting and writing while my friends and family toiled at menial jobs that were physically more demanding than mine and were barely making ends meet. I knew I was viewed as the one who got out of "the hood." And I didn't want people to think that I thought I was better than them or "uppity." So, to prove how down I was, I would often front the bill for everyone. I bought computers, gave down payments for homes, paid for holidays, concert tickets, etc. And yes, it was nice to have the financial means to help my friends and family, but I was also setting up a very costly dynamic that made me feel they only loved me for my money. It was a lonely feeling.

We often hear about basketball players, rappers, and entertainers who are estranged from their families. Usually, money is the root of the problem—someone gave too much, and someone thought it wasn't enough. Sound familiar?

I eventually learned how to set financial boundaries with my family, and it was hard. The first time I said no was to a family member who demanded I lend them $40,000 to put down on a house. The fallout was quick, and they stopped talking to me for months. I also set up a rule that I would give money only as a gift, not a loan, and I had to think hard about whether I could afford to give it away. I also had to learn that I did not need to donate to every single cause or GoFundMe request that came across my desk. I did experience some backlash, but I was very clear that it was my money, and I could choose where I wanted to spend it. You have a right to spend your money the way you want to.

SIS, DON'T GIVE 'EM YOUR MONEY—YET!
WHEN FOLKS ASK YOU FOR MONEY, DO THE FOLLOWING:

Take your time. Twenty-four hours is a good amount of time to sit and think. Do not get caught up in "Tyrone's emergency"—it can wait. Someone's emergency is not your emergency.

What is your history with them pertaining to money? Do they constantly ask you for money? Have you given them money before? Have they paid you back? Do they actually have the means to pay you back within a reasonable time? If not, are you in a financial position to see this as a gift?

Is there another way you can support them? Can you offer to look after their children while they job hunt? Can you pay for their groceries for a month to ease their financial burden? Can you help them create a budget? Sometimes support does not always have to be financial. How can you emotionally support them?

Be okay with the fallout. Not everyone is going to be okay with you telling them no. Folks are going to get mad. They may even stop talking to you. You may want to adopt the policy that you no longer lend money, so folks know not to ask. You need to be very clear and treat everyone equally, no exceptions. Even Oprah Winfrey talks about how she had to learn to stop being her family's ATM and say no to folks who thought they had a right to her money. If Oprah, who is worth billions of dollars, can say it's time to set some financial boundaries, I think it's time you do!

MY FINANCIAL COME-TO-JESUS MOMENT!

Sis, I'm going to get really deep with you. Even with all the knowledge I had about success, guilt, and setting boundaries with family and friends about money, I still had an unhealthy dynamic with money. I still lay awake at night in my upper-middle-class home with the double car garage in a neighborhood that looked similar to Raquel's parents' Stonegate neighborhood. I felt I had made it, yet I still felt like a fraud. And no matter what I did, I could not get rid of my shame and angst around money.

So it was no surprise that the Universe felt a need to send me my biggest lesson about money. I will call her "Success Story," because she was indeed a self-made, highly educated woman with money. On our first date, "Success Story" showed up in a fancy, fully loaded luxury car. Promptly she told me she was a woman of means. Suddenly, I was embarrassed by my small Nissan Versa that was fully paid off and drove perfectly well. Two months into our relationship, I traded in my car for my first luxury vehicle, a drop top BMW. Our relationship progressed and included fancy vacations and five-star restaurants. And even though I was making great money, I was fully aware that my new girlfriend made nearly four times my salary. I was finding it hard to keep pace with her spending, and the disparity between our incomes concerned me. But every time I tried to broach the subject, she said I worried too much and that she enjoyed spending money on me and taking on most of the financial responsibility. She assured me that "for once, I needed to let someone take care of me." So, I relaxed into it. It was nice for once to not be the frightened little girl in bed worried about being homeless. I now had a successful, rich fiancée—a self-made millionaire. I thought all my prayers were being answered.

We decided to move in together and combine our lives and resources. I ignored that little voice that said the luxury apartment we chose was not a good idea—it was nearly three times the amount of my modest mortgage. I kept hearing the stern Jamaican voice of my grandmother inside my head. "Mek [make]sure you put your basket where you can reach it!" I was putting my basket way out of my reach. My basket wasn't even in the same room as me; it was on another planet! This apartment was too expensive!

My stomach was in knots. I tried to convince myself that I should count my blessings because these trappings of success signaled to me that I had finally made it. But the Universe kept speaking to me even though I refused to listen. One day I overheard her on the phone saying that I had only a basic understanding of money, and she was surprised I had made it this far in life. I was hurt, but I never told her I had heard what she said.

My shame was now taking up full residence in my life. My biggest fear had come true. Someone had discovered that I really didn't belong in the "club for the rich." I started to depend on her even more. I barely recognized myself. No longer was I the fiercely independent, confident woman I had once been. I was now someone who had no clue what was going on financially in her household. I had given up my power. Yet I ignored all the signs.

And I thought I had no right to complain or ask anything of her because, essentially, she was paying the majority of our household expenses. While the relationship provided me with financial stability, part of me thought that it lacked emotional depth and vulnerability. A friend tried to warn me that money doesn't fix everything. I ignored the advice. I knew I deserved more, but I was unsure how to ask for it without possibly appearing ungrateful. I felt like the scared little broke girl trapped inside the beautiful palace. I was in love, I wanted this to work, and I was also invested. Invested in the image of being part of a power couple. Invested in the dream that my little girl needed to see come true. And, honestly, I didn't want to worry about money anymore. The thought of leaving and starting all over again with someone else made me weary. So I basically slammed the door on the Universe's warnings. And as my biggest mentor, Oprah, gracefully put it, "Life whispers to you all the time. It whispers, and if you don't get the whisper, the whisper gets louder. If you don't get the whisper when it gets louder, I call it like a little pebble—a little thump—upside the head. The pebble or the thump upside the head usually means it's gone into a problem. If you don't pay attention to the problem, the pebble then becomes like a brick. The brick upside your head is a crisis, and if you don't pay attention to the brick upside your head, the crisis turns into a disaster and the whole house—brick wall—comes falling down . . ." And indeed, my whole house came crumbling down when my fiancée texted me to end the relationship.

So why did this happen to me? I pondered this over many sleepless nights. It would have been easy to make my fiancée the villain in this story, but I know I also played my significant part. My money shame came to haunt me because I had never fully dealt with it. All my life, I had been running from it, and it finally caught up with me. All my fears of being thrown out on the street and not having enough money to survive had come true.

This humbling and humiliating experience forced me to take an honest and hard look at my life. I started to look at not only my current situation but also my past.

THAT FRIGHTENED LITTLE BLACK GIRL

I knew I needed to sit down with that little girl and fully address my money shame. I knew there was a message in this for myself and others. Yes, my mess was going to be my message.

I also needed to take ownership of my part in the ending of our relationship. I had given away my power. I had silenced my voice. I had regressed to a child because I was so desperate for someone to take care of me and didn't believe I was fully capable of doing those things for myself. I had made her the parent in the relationship because as a child I had experienced constant money insecurity. Now as an adult I was seeking security. I had given her full financial authority in our relationship because I believed she knew more about money than I did, which meant she was more worthy, more powerful, and essentially "better" than me. I did not show up in this relationship as a fully actualized, successful, independent adult who was a big fucking deal! Instead I stood in awe of her, thinking that I was "lucky" that someone like her had chosen this poor little girl from the hood.

While I sat with these painful revelations, I quietly packed up my entire life in 12 cardboard boxes. (Yes, I counted them because I wanted this to be a reminder that I could live simply and take only what's important.) I did not have the energy to look for a new apartment while packing up my old apartment, looking after a newborn, and mourning the demise of my dream relationship. So I put my 12 boxes into storage and humbly moved back in with my mother and assisted my sister with her plans for her dream wedding. I was hurt, embarrassed, and devastated. My life was in shambles.

After doing some internal work and finding an apartment within my means, I started to educate myself about money. I found a financial planner, and I bought life insurance. I listened to audiobooks about money. I joined the Live Richer Academy, an online service created by Tiffany Aliche, a Black woman whose mission is to educate other women about wealth. I vowed to take one class per week, where I learned about budgets, stocks, and real estate among other topics. Armed with this information, I created a budget. I began reciting money affirmations daily, reading financial books, and watching financial shows on YouTube. I started to invest in stocks and educate myself on real estate investing. I learned from this disaster. I examined my family's financial past and present—the good and the bad—and became certain that I could change our financial narrative.

Every day, I became a little bit stronger, and my son became another incentive to complete this life lesson. I don't want him to grow up with financial insecurity. I wanted to be able to confidently provide for my family. I was no longer the little girl afraid of being kicked out on the street. I had survived the worst, and I was able to take care of myself. I came out stronger, wiser, kinder, and more confident about who I was and what I would allow to show up in my life.

SIS, GET YOUR MIND RIGHT!

Take a deep breath. Consider meditating before starting this exercise.

1. Write down your money story starting with these questions: What did the conversations about money look like in your household? Was there enough money? Were you keeping up with the Joneses? Was your family living above their means? What did your father and mother teach you about money?

2. How do you currently view money? Does it solve all problems? Is it the root of all evil? Is money supposed to be shared or hoarded?

3. Now write yourself an honest letter. Write down the relationship you would like to have with money. Address any success guilt that you may have.

4. Make a list of your monthly bills and compare it with your monthly income. Are you living below or above your means?

5. Highlight any unexpected surprises in your budget. Are you giving money away to family and friends to make them love you? Are you spending a lot of money eating out?

A JOURNEY WITH NO FINAL DESTINATION

I'm still on an intense journey when it comes to money. Sometimes fear creeps in, and I start to panic about whether I will have enough money. And if I will die broke. But during those times, I become softer with myself. I name it. I welcome it. I address it. Then I write down what I'm feeling, the things I'm grateful for, and what areas of my life are evidence of abundance. So I will give thanks for having money to pay all my bills on time. For having extra money to give to a homeless person. Or having enough money to send to a friend who may be experiencing a hard time. Or having friends who will randomly send me boxes of diapers and formula. Or having a beautiful outdoor patio space I can write from. Sometimes, it's as simple as saying I'm grateful for just waking up this morning. All these things are evidence of abundance in my life and how the Universe always takes care of me. After I finish my gratitude journal, I will often do a visualization exercise. To do this, you can lie down or sit cross-legged. I like to play soft spa-like music, but you can also do the visualization without music. In my mind, I picture myself sitting at a desk reading my bank statement, which reflects that I have lots of money. More money than

I can ever imagine in my lifetime. I also picture myself receiving numerous checks. My favorite visualization is when I picture myself living in my dream home, and my entire family and several friends are there with me. We are happy, peaceful, and everyone is laughing. And I'm delighted that I can afford such a beautiful home to host them. Throughout my day I often find myself returning to this image and it always brings me joy and comfort.

Also, money affirmations have helped me. If you need to address money blocks in your life, I recommend writing out money affirmations daily, at least 7–10 times, especially if you have identified this as an area where you feel "stuck." Usually, I pick one affirmation to say throughout the day at random times. I also have a money affirmation as the screen saver on my phone. Following is a list of affirmations I have used:

affirmations

I DELIGHT IN THE FINANCIAL SECURITY
THAT IS CONSTANT IN MY LIFE.

THE LORD IS MY SHEPHERD, I HAVE NO LACK.

I AM OPEN AND RECEPTIVE TO ALL
THE WEALTH IN THE UNIVERSE.

ABUNDANCE IS MINE NOW.

MY CUP OVERFLOWS WITH DAILY BLESSINGS.

I AM ALWAYS BLESSED, AND ALL MY
NEEDS ARE ALWAYS MET.

LIFE SUPPORTS ME IN EVERY WAY!

RICHES AND RICHES ARE AN
EVERYDAY EXPERIENCE FOR ME.

I AM COMMITTED TO CHANGING
MY FAMILY'S WEALTH STORY.
A NEW MONEY LEGACY BEGINS WITH ME!

chapter 6

Sis Works Hard for the Money

BLACK GIRL PLAYLIST:
"I AM NOT MY HAIR,"
INDIA ARIE

"If you want to know about a black woman, touch her hair, 'cause that's where we carry all our hurts, hopes, dreams, disappointments."

—NOVELETTE, *'DA KINK IN MY HAIR*

On Shonda Rhimes's show *Scandal*, when Rowan Pope reminded his defiant daughter, Olivia Pope, about their family motto, "You have to be twice as good as them to get half of what they have," there was a collective murmur as we nodded our heads at the TV screen. I don't think there is a Black woman alive whose mama, daddy, or grand-daddy didn't give them some variation of that motto.

Yet working twice as hard has really done a number on our health. While we are putting in double or triple overtime, many of us have neglected our health and well-being to prove that we deserved to be in the room. My first job in the industry was as an intern on *The Chris Rock Show*. Out of five interns, only two of us were Black. I knew that to stand out, I needed to outwork everyone. So, I would get to the office at least two hours before our start time, ensuring I was there to start the coffee and get the newspapers ready for the writing team. I happily took on more work and assignments than the other interns, and when the rest of the interns packed up to catch the 5 P.M. train, I would stay behind, waiting for the last writer to leave. Sometimes, I wouldn't leave until 10 P.M. And yes, my hard work paid off. I eventually got showcased in a small sketch and also worked as a writer's assistant and an assistant in the audience department. And the skills I developed there were invaluable, but I often think back to how exhausted I was. I was supplying a lot of unpaid labor, and money concerns were an issue for me. I was sharing a bachelor's apartment with three other people—with the cockroaches taking up more room than any of us! Having very little money added to my stress, and I was unable to buy nutritious foods. On many nights, I ate hotdogs because I couldn't afford to buy groceries. Also, I failed to factor in that I was a twentysomething young girl heading home really late at night by myself, and at the time I never even considered how dangerous that was. All to show I was a hard worker and deserved to be there.

NO ONE LOOKS LIKE ME.

Most of us know that the higher up we go in life and the more prestigious our job, the less we see faces that look like us. And no matter how hard we work and all the sacrifices we make, we still question whether or not we deserve to be there.

I told you guys that my sister has a Ph.D. in Math. (Yes, my mother just pops out overachieving children!) After graduation, my sister was scouted by many corporations and organizations. Eventually, she accepted an offer from a top cancer research institute. She called me one day, hurt and outraged, and shared a humiliating story. She was attending a conference, and at dinner, one of her colleagues, in front of a large group, asserted that it must have been easier for her to get into school because she was a "diverse candidate" and her success was directly linked to universities having to fulfill their diversity quota. My sister was speechless. In one fell swoop, he had completely dismissed all the hard work and sacrifices she had made. Here she was at dinner with a table of white men, and none of them made any sort of acknowledgment about how their own privilege and "blue blood" may have led to many doors being open to them. Should I mention the college scandal where many elite white families got busted for paying their children's way in? Yet, as Black women, we have to constantly defend accusations about being "diversity hires" or "equity quotas."

And this is the story of many successful Black women: we have to sit with the judgment and the assumption that we only got to where we are because of affirmative action. When I asked my sister how she responded, she admitted that she took a deep breath and politely smiled and said nothing.

When shooting *'Da Kink in My Hair,* a young, bubbly blonde woman was assigned to work with the co-creator and me to help execute our vision of the show. I'll call her "Karen." Karen had more television experience than the two of us combined, and we were actually relieved that we had someone who was going to walk us through the process. Yet a few weeks in, we realized that "Houston, we have a problem." Every time we had a difference of opinion, Karen would burst into tears and express that she didn't feel heard. In every interaction with her, I would deliberately change my tone to a high, non-threatening singing soprano. Sometimes I felt as if I were auditioning for a part in *The Sound of Music.* But Karen would still tear up, and her nose would turn red. So I changed tactics and tried speaking barely above a whisper. This seemed to upset Karen even more. No matter what I did, Karen was committed to crying nearly every day.

It didn't take long before the network dragged our Black asses into a meeting. Two young Black women sat across the table from three white TV executives who basically held our fate in their hands. They expressed that they were holding an emergency meeting because Karen found us "intimidating." They encouraged us to let Karen do her job and be team players. We politely nodded and did not even try to defend ourselves because we knew that one word from us would cause us to be perceived as "Angry Black Women." We were also fully aware that they had the power to take away our show, and the financial impact of that was not lost on us. We knew how important this show was to so many Black and Brown people. Many people were counting on our show for their livelihood. We also knew that because we were the "first" Black women in Canada to have a TV show, if we didn't make this work, the opportunity might never be given to another Black person. So we just swallowed our words and our bubbling rage.

After the meeting, my co-creator and I went to my dressing room to debrief. We were so thankful that we had each other to go over the craziness of the situation. In the dressing room, we laughed and we cried. Both of us knew that to survive this, we needed to hang on tight to each other. We decided then and there that we needed to present a united front, and we needed to mentally and emotionally check in with each other each day because it was obvious that no one had our backs, and we needed to create a safe place for each other.

Often, when I'm coaching successful women who are at the top of their game, I advise them to intentionally find other Black women within their organization or company to be their confidants and sounding board. If finding other Black women is not possible, they must actively seek Black women outside of their job to vent with. We need someone who can fully hear us, see us, and believe us. It is not enough to think that you alone can handle all the foolishness we are subjected to every day. I also strongly suggest finding a Black therapist, someone who you can vent to weekly—do not walk around with all this pent-up anger and hurt. When we do not seek support, it can lead to depression.

We have been raised to keep our heads up. We are raised to not let them see us cry. Yet every day, structural and systemic racism and dealing with the constant stress of being a Black woman can wear you down, physically and emotionally. I refer to it as "Black Fatigue." The daily tax we pay for just being Black. The unfair scrutiny placed on us, the constant threat we have on our lives, our children's lives. Getting up when everything in our body screams that we need to rest and stay in bed. Swallowing our anger at our jobs because we don't want to be labeled as angry, defensive, or intimidating. From shopping while Black and being followed around stores to a Karen reaching out to touch our hair at the water cooler, being a Black woman can get tiring. We don't always fully acknowledge how these things can slowly chip away at our soul. And we smile through our hurt. So many of us can recall leaving a team meeting and going into the bathroom stall to cry. Meanwhile, Karen had a full-blown meltdown at the team meeting, and we forced a sympathetic smile as we handed her the Kleenex box.

Working while Black is highly stressful and taking care of our mental health should be our utmost priority.

DEALING WITH EVERYDAY MICROAGGRESSIONS

My cousin, with great humor, related at a family dinner how often the white women at her office would ask questions about her hair and be so fascinated with her ability to change her hairstyles. Their probing questions ranged from "Is your hair real?" and "Do you wash your hair?" to "Can I touch it?" And even though we all giggled, I could not miss the tired look in my cousin's eyes about literally being the "pet" in her workplace. It wasn't fair that she had to field questions that would never be asked of her white counterparts. And if she didn't answer with a smile, she would be viewed as defensive or difficult.

I have a friend who is a doctor who shared that she had gotten used to being called the nurse whenever she went into a patient's room, even though she was wearing a white coat. With a wry smile, she told of clearly introducing herself as the doctor, speaking to the patient about their various ailments, and the patient politely thanking her and then promptly inquiring when the doctor would be in. When I asked her how this made her feel, she brushed it off and said it comes with the territory. Many times, as Black women, we brush off these "little things" and do not adequately address how they start to add up and take a toll on our mental and physical health.

SIS, GET YOUR MIND RIGHT!

1. Take a look at your workplace/work environment. What additional supports can you put in place to ensure that you feel supported at work?

2. What you can do for your emotional health and well-being when you have a stressful day at work? Some ideas: calling a friend or taking a walk.

3. Enroll in an online business group that is geared toward professional women so you can have more built-in support. I truly recommend *Support Is Sexy* founded by powerhouse Elayne Fluker.

affirmations

I HAVE NO OBSTACLES, ONLY MAJOR OPPORTUNITIES IN MY LIFE AND MY WORK.

I AM SO HAPPY TO BE WORKING IN MY DREAM JOB.

I AM SO PASSIONATE ABOUT THE WORK THAT I DO.

chapter 7

Sis, Can We Talk Therapy?

BLACK GIRL PLAYLIST:
"THERAPY,"
MARY J. BLIGE

*"I wish you were as compassionate
to yourself as you are to others."*

—MY BLACK THERAPIST

Therapy is spoken about in our community in hushed tones. It is viewed as something that only white girls do. You must be really mad or really soft if you're going to therapy. And God knows why you're going to tell all your business to some white person. Black folks, we ain't about that life. When I first told my family I was seeing a therapist, my mother nearly spat out her mouthful of rice and peas! "Gyal, you don't have nothing better to do with yu money; yu must tink you're white!"

There is a stigma about therapy in our community and therefore a strong resistance to it. However, things are changing as many high-profile celebrity women are talking about going to therapy. Actress and producer Issa Rae, from the hit TV show *Insecure*, talks about the pressure of being a Black woman in Hollywood and why that made it imperative for her to seek professional help. "You're just a ticket for the next project. Or you're a to-do list item for them. They're [the entertainment industry] not worried about how you're doing. They mean well, but nobody really cares. So it's only on you to make sure you're good."

I have also been very open on social media about therapy. I even created a series on my Instagram called "My Black Therapist said," where I offer quotes and advice that my therapist has actually offered in my sessions. Because of that, I've received many inquiries from other Black women about referrals and resources. Many women have shared that they have tried therapy in the past and were not fully satisfied with the experience because often, the woman sitting across from them was white and could not fully understand the layered complexities of being a Black woman. In the past, many of my therapists failed to fully comprehend the intersectionalities of my life. I was Black, queer, and female. And even though they were sympathetic and offered solid advice, I often left my session feeling as if something was missing. It wasn't until I actively sought out a Black therapist that my therapy experience drastically changed. There was a shorthand in our interactions that was missing in past experiences. It gave me a true sense of belonging and being fully seen. I would strongly encourage you to seek out a Black therapist. You'll find a list of resources at the back of this book. Therapy used to be expensive, but now there are so many ways to access therapy that can fit any size budget.

I believe if you are committed to your well-being and honestly want to be a Black girl in love (with herself), finding a good therapist should be at the top of your list.

> What to look for in a therapist and some questions to ask:
>
> • Have you worked with women of color before and specifically Black women?
>
> • What are your thoughts on intersectionality and how it impacts Black women?
>
> • What is your experience of dealing with people of diverse sexualities?
>
> • Do you accept insurance or offer a sliding scale for your clients?

DEPRESSION/ANXIETY

I once overheard my grandmother gossiping about another relative and stating, "Well, you know she has bad nerves, nervous like a kitten. So you have to take it easy on her." Later, as an adult, I realized the relative they were talking about struggled with depression and anxiety. Many women in my family struggled with their mental health. I have aunts and cousins who had full breakdowns and were in and out of psychiatric hospitals. Yet there were many whose subtle mental health struggles went undiagnosed or undetected. As a child, I witnessed my grandmother heading to bed in the middle of the day. She would draw the curtains, pull the blankets over her head, and not come out of her room for days. During those times, we would not disturb her, and everyone knew that we needed to make as little noise as possible. I would tiptoe into her room and leave a small cup of tea on her dresser, and only her heavy sighing under the covers would indicate to me that she was still alive. Sometimes I could hear her muttering under the sheets, "I'm just so fed up." After a few days, my grandmother would miraculously emerge and be full of vigor and optimism. As a family, we never spoke about this, and it wasn't until I started writing this book and began reflecting on what mental health looked like within my own family that I recalled those episodes.

In many Black families, we avoid naming what is going on. If we name it, we are forced to deal with it. When I was going through my devastating breakup and crying every day with barely enough energy to get out of bed, my sister and mother dutifully gathered around me and silently helped me with the daily duties of trying to live my life and raise my son. No one directly addressed my mental health. After three months of crying nonstop and being able to do just the bare minimum, I had to face that something was wrong with me. This was more than grieving the demise of a relationship. Eventually I connected with an online support group for adoptive mothers, and there I learned about adoptive mothers suffering from postpartum depression. I didn't know it was possible for that to happen to adoptive mothers. After reading all the symptoms, I knew I was definitely experiencing something similar, so I shared the news with my mother.

Me: "I think I'm depressed. I may have postpartum depression."

My mother, without missing a beat: "Of course, you're depressed. Everybody knows that! But you'll be fine."

I was shocked. How come no one told me, and why did none of my family encourage me to seek medical attention or support? After that exchange, my mother began washing the dishes, which meant the conversation was over. After connecting with several other Black women about our experiences with depression, many shared that the conversation I had with my mother was similar to the conversation or "non-conversation" that occurred in their own families. We are unwilling to name and say aloud things such as depression and anxiety because we do not want another label placed on us that can add to our hardship. It's hard enough being a Black woman. Add being depressed, and that is another hurdle to overcome.

I wanted to get more insight into our reluctance to name mental health within our community, so I interviewed Dr. Angela Neal-Barnett, psychologist and author of *Soothe Your Nerves: The Black Woman's Guide to Understanding and Overcoming Anxiety, Panic, and Fear*. She shared that our community just doesn't have the vocabulary to name it or talk about it—so, we can't talk about it without being labeled as crazy. And there is a huge distinction between experiencing anxiety and depression and being mentally ill. I asked her to explain the difference between anxiety and depression because I had been using both terms interchangeably. Based on our conversation, I've come up with a list of questions that can help determine if you are suffering from depression and anxiety.

Anxiety:

- When you think about the future, do you feel like something bad is going to happen?

- Do you ever experience panic attacks?

- Are you uncomfortable in social settings? If so, do you avoid them?

- Do you isolate yourself?

- Do you ever experience sleep paralysis?

Depression:

- Do you feel sad and irritable for periods of two weeks or more?

- Do these extremes apply to you?

    - You overeat or don't eat at all.

    - You sleep a lot or don't sleep at all.

- Would you say you have low energy?

- Are your moods interfering with your life and stopping you from doing what you need to do?

- Do you ever wonder what your life would be like if you didn't feel the way you do?

According to Dr. Neal-Barnett, Black women who consider themselves religious have difficulty admitting they have depression and anxiety or even seeking treatment. Something else preventing us from seeking help is our belief that we can make it through because we are strong and to be weak as a Black woman is an oxymoron. By the time we finally seek treatment, our symptoms have grown more severe. The other barrier to accessing support is resources. If we do not have health insurance or money to pursue treatment, praying or taking it to God seems like a cheaper alternative.

I nodded as I recalled how many times, when the pressure became too much for me, I was encouraged by well-meaning family and friends to bring it to the Lord and *"Girl, pray on it!"* The Black community has used the church as our safe haven and salvation. And indeed, the church has continued to be an integral pillar of support for many of us. And yes, attending church and praying is a valid tool, but it shouldn't be the only tool we use in our mental health toolbox. Our issues and stress are too complex and layered to only seek one option. We should implement a practice of several mental health options.

Here I was, interviewing a doctor about why Black women would not seek help, and I knew the reason I didn't want to seek help was that I did not want to be viewed as weak. I was running away from addressing my own emotional struggles. I shared with my mother that I thought I was depressed, but I chose to explore natural remedies and decided a holistic approach was my first step. Yoga and meditation did help alleviate some of my symptoms, but while interviewing the doctor, I couldn't help but think I was one of those women who was living with her symptoms longer than necessary. I was still crying every day, sometimes three to four times per day (not an exaggeration), and I struggled with trying to lift this dark fog that clouded my thoughts. I had not slept in days and my brain didn't want to shut down. And what really worried me was that I couldn't shrug off an overall feeling of hopelessness. Doing everyday things such as washing the dishes, bathing my son, writing, and just getting out of bed felt hard, but I pushed myself because my son was counting on me, I had bills that needed to be paid, and I needed to finish this book. After talking with Dr. Neal-Barnett, I knew I needed to be much more intentional about seeking medical and emotional support, which I did shortly after.

So, sis, in my first draft of this book, I ended the chapter at the last sentence you just read. Yeah, girl, that was supposed to be it! But I knew I was deliberately not saying what I needed to say. The part of the story that I tried to "gloss" over or not write at all is when I received my own professional diagnosis of depression. I wasn't sure if I was ready to share it with the world. I could hear my granny's voice saying, "Don't tell everybody your business!" But I know that my story may save another woman's life.

When I hung up the phone with Dr. Neal-Barnett, I could no longer deny that I was experiencing depression. I truly thought it was a passing phase and at first playfully referred to it as my "breakup slump." I tried to convince myself that yoga, meditation, and journaling would be enough. And they helped to some degree, but I knew there was something wrong. I had all the clinical signs of depression that the doctor had mentioned. Yet they were more extreme. I knew she was right when she said that often Black women do not seek treatment until their symptoms are severe. I was the Black woman she was talking about. I could no longer deny it. I needed professional help.

I sought out an online psychiatrist and scheduled an appointment for the next week. On our Zoom call he asked about my family history, and I shared with him the mental health history of my family. The list was long. I also shared all my symptoms and the most recent traumatic events in my life, including a major breakup, a move, a new baby, and mothering in a pandemic. He looked at me in disbelief and said that just ONE of these things could cause major stress and emotional dysfunction in an individual's life and here I was trying to desperately cope with several major life-changing events with very little support. He asked why I had taken so long to seek help. I shamefully admitted, "I thought I could handle it." He immediately prescribed me an anti-depressant and a sleep aid for my insomnia. He then scheduled a follow-up appointment with a counselor and told me he would personally be following up with me in three months. I told him that would not be necessary, and that I'm sure I only need to be on medication for a few weeks. He shook his head as he explained I needed more than a few weeks for the medication to work. He then said, "Trey, I strongly advise that you take the medication for longer. Be prepared to be on this medication for at least a year or more. You are severely depressed."

A few days later, when my medication arrived, I stared at the box with suspicion and it sat on my kitchen counter for five days. I didn't want to take medication. I didn't want to be labeled as someone who has depression. And worst of all, I didn't want to think of myself as "weak" or someone who was too "delicate" to handle her own life. But I knew that I could not continue on this downward spiral. I lovingly told myself it was okay to seek help and that taking medication didn't mean that I was weak. My hands shook as I popped a pill in my mouth. Within three weeks of consistently taking my medication I noticed a drastic difference. All of my symptoms were gone. I was sleeping, thinking more clearly, and the world seemed brighter. I had more energy. I started feeling like my old self and I knew I had made the right choice. However, I still had so much shame around this, so I didn't tell anyone that I was on medication. Yet this all changed on one fateful morning.

It was 4 a.m. and my son had woken up two hours early. Half asleep, I headed to the kitchen to make him a bottle. While feeding him I reached for my phone and jumped on Facebook and was immediately notified that a friend was streaming live. I thought it was odd to be doing this at 4:15 in the morning but I clicked on it and was the only one in the chat. My friend was incoherent and crying and in obvious distress. I was able to make out a few words before realizing that I was watching a suicidal person use their social media platform to say goodbye to friends and family. I typed out a frantic message. *"Please don't do this! I know things feel heavy right now. Trust me I know how you feel! Please give me a call!"* But my friend ignored my messages and quickly logged off. I immediately sprang into action, calling numerous friends and then the police. Several hours later I was given an update by the police. Thankfully it was a happy ending. My friend was in the hospital receiving the support they desperately needed. But I was shaken. I knew there were many people like my friend and myself who were suffering in silence. A few days later I called my friend, who had just been released from the hospital, and they told me that they had stopped taking their medication because they didn't think they needed it anymore. I paused and with a deep breath shared that I also suffered from depression and I was on medication. They were in shock. "YOU!!???? But you seem to have it all together!" I laughed, "I do but I'm also depressed!" We both shared our feelings about the stigma around depression, our resistance to taking medication, our collective shame. After our call I knew that I had to share with others so they would know they weren't alone. I slowly started to reveal to my inner circle that I was taking medication for depression. I was surprised by the reaction. Many shared their own struggles with depression and anxiety. Another superstar/powerhouse friend confessed that she had attempted suicide twice! Several high-power sistahs in my circle told me in hushed voices about their ongoing battle with depression and mental health. I was shocked by how many of us were fighting our own demons. Fighting in isolation. Sistahs reached out to share they often felt unsafe or too ashamed to admit their personal struggles. I knew then that it was important for me to be visible with my own struggles to help create a safe place for other Black women to share theirs and to use my platform to advocate for Black women and our mental health.

MANY OF US STILL SUFFER IN SILENCE

In my own recovery I'm reminded of a dear friend of mine who would go missing for several weeks at a time. She would stop answering calls, texts, and e-mail, and then out of nowhere, she would pop back up and say that she just got "busy." After several years of this behavior, I put my foot down. I told her I thought she did not value our friendship, and in my time of need, she was often conveniently missing in action. I yelled, "This friendship is over! You don't value me!"

My friend listened, and then in a quiet, shaky voice she said, "Trey, I suffer from depression. When I go missing, it's because I can't deal with anything or anyone."

I was speechless. We had been friends for nearly 15 years, and she had never told me this. Why didn't she feel safe enough to share this with me? And how come I didn't recognize the signs? I realized it's because I had always viewed her as this charismatic, ambitious, highly successful woman. A Black woman who had her shit together!

And yes, she was still all those things, but she was also a woman who was suffering in silence with depression. I felt guilty for being so self-absorbed that I didn't realize one of my closest friends was struggling emotionally. I vowed, moving forward, to do an emotional check-in with my friends and ask them how they are doing and truly listen to what they say.

Dr. Neal-Barnett told me, "Depression and anxiety are treatable, and you can reclaim your life!"

I have successfully reclaimed my life!

So, sis, let go of the shame and stigma, and please go seek the help you need.

Following are some daily things and practices that can enhance your mental health. And if you think you need additional support, please seek professional help.

MEDITATION

I did not jump on the meditation bandwagon willingly. It was a bit woo-woo for me. I wasn't completely sold on the idea that all I needed to do was a light a candle, hold hands in a circle with a couple of barefoot blonde women in Lululemon pants, breathe, and everything would be well in my life. Okay . . . But then I couldn't help noticing that every time someone I deeply admired spoke about their life and success, they would mention that meditation was a part of their daily practice. Once I heard famous Black women like Tina Turner, Oprah Winfrey, Beyoncé, Halle Berry, Alice Walker, and Michelle Obama talking about meditation, I knew I needed to perhaps go light a candle.

So I decided I needed to master this meditation thang because if Oprah says it's a game changer, well, ain't nobody arguing with Oprah! When I first started to meditate, I would often fall asleep or my brain would not stop racing through my long to-do list. I thought meditation was a waste of time, and I couldn't figure out what all the hype was about. Eventually, I found success using guiding meditation, during which someone guided me through the practice, helping me stay focused. I went from doing 10-minute meditations to meditating 30 to 45 minutes per day.

Implementing a daily practice of meditation has calmed down my overthinking. Meditation has helped me slow down my mind and gain more clarity. I even sleep better. So, girl, give it a chance and don't give up if the first time feels awkward. It took me nearly a year to figure out what really worked for me, and now I can't live without it.

EXERCISE

I'm going to be straight with you. If God came down to earth and told me, "Trey, you can eat whatever you want, and you will never get thigh rub. I'll take away your back fat, and you will never gain a pound!" I'm telling you I would never exercise another day in my life! I hate exercising! Yet, if I didn't work out, I would never fit into my favorite jeans and my stomach would cover three zip codes. I have zero metabolism, and I love to eat. I have a sweet tooth—I love chocolates, cakes, and scones with fresh whipped cream. And a fresh loaf of bread slathered in butter has nearly brought me to orgasm! Because I know these truths about myself, I work out so I can keep my weight in check. I'm barely five feet tall, and I know what it is like to carry 240 pounds on my small frame. When I dropped nearly 90 pounds, it changed my life. And I'm not here to fat shame anyone, so keep your damn fat or phat activism to yourself! Girl, I've been there, so I'm on your side, and I'm far from a size zero! I'm fully aware of how the world responds to women who do not fit a typical beauty standard. For me, dropping the weight made me feel better physically and emotionally. But if holding on to the belief that "I'm just big boned" is making you live your best life, girl, keep doing you! But for me, it wasn't working. So to keep me somewhat happy with that chick looking back at me in the mirror and keep me fitting into my snug "best life" jeans, and because I only want to wear one pair of Spanx (the last time I wore two, I nearly collapsed on stage), I try to make exercise a daily part of my routine.

But I'm not a gym rat. Going to the gym or working out involves a self-barter system that goes like this: "Trey, if you go to the gym today, you can binge-watch all of *Temptation Island* tonight!" Or "If you go to the gym, you can eat a chicken roti and two pieces of plantain!"

Hiking and walking are my favorite things. I try to walk at least 30 minutes or more every day. I love going on long hikes, and to give my endurance an extra boost, I do spin workouts. I strongly encourage you to find a form of physical exercise that works for you and implement it for 30 minutes or more, three to five times per week. After being diagnosed with depression I started jogging and I now I do it six days per week. I love it! I listen to my favorite hip-hop station and I'm transported to another world, where I'm better than the best, and I'm slaying at all things—isn't that what most rappers say? When I jog, my brain seems to slow down. I get into a meditative state and I'm able to take long deep breaths and remind myself to take life one step at a time. Jogging has contributed to my overall well-being. I never thought I would be one of those women running through the neighborhood with a jogging stroller, hair bouncing in a ponytail, wearing black Lululemon leggings—but girl, I'm now that chick! Correction: that BLACK CHICK. However, my leggings are from Target! Just keeping it real. Exercise is a great stress reliever, and it's something you can do that only benefits you. You deserve it. And yes, you have the time!!!

GIRL, GO ON AND GET YOUR HAIR DID!

Getting your hair done can definitely lift your spirits, and I deliberately placed this paragraph after the exercise advice because many of us avoid exercise due to worry about sweating out our blowout or messing up our laid edges. When I first started doing hot yoga, I had to choose between being toned and flexible or looking like a hot mess! Because the heat wreaked havoc on my hair, I thought about giving up on my classes, but I could not deny how much it was helping my mental health. I eventually resorted to some protective styles that sometimes made me look like Celie from *The Color Purple*. When I wasn't doing hot yoga, something that definitely lifted my spirits was going to the hairdresser.

The hair salon is our sanctuary. And I love it. Damn, I made an entire career out of talking about Black women, our hair, and our love affair with our hairdresser. Both *'Da Kink in My Hair* play and television show was based on my own childhood experience of visiting the hair salon that my aunt owned. Only at the salon can you get the latest and low-down gossip on who's dating whose husband. And then there's Little Nicky rushing in with his fine self. He's so fine but so broke! And he's trying to sell you his latest CD *again*. And of course you always rummage around in your bag and fish out a crumpled $10 to help support an enterprising brotha! And now there's somebody's momma parking her food truck right outside the joint, music blaring. You rush out with the plastic bonnet still on your head to grab some jerk chicken or smoked ribs.

A Black girl's experience at the hairdresser is like no other. When I go to the hairdresser it's confessional time for me. And some of us definitely use our hairdresser as a stand-in therapist. (But as good as your hairdresser is, girl, you still need to find a therapist!) My hairdresser knows all my secrets, and she's going to be the one who writes the tell-all book about my life! And she's also a magician! Somehow, she can take me from hot mess to cover girl in a few short hours. . . okay, six long hours! But four of them are spent waiting on her late ass while she's arguing on the phone! And as you patiently sit there you swear that you ain't ever coming back because she's trifling! But week after week, there you are, waiting on her magic! But I digress. . .

I loved seeing my locs in intricate spirals. Throw in some red highlights, and all of a sudden, my day just got brighter! the hair salon can be a healing place. Tender hands on our scalps, being surrounded by women who look like us and understand us, jokes and advice bouncing off the walls. So, I encourage you to go and look after *'Da Kink in My Hair* (see what I did there?) if you want to look and feel better about yourself.

JOURNALING

Girl, write that shit down! I was given my first journal at age 12, and I love looking back on some of my old journals to witness my growth. Journaling is also a living testament to the saying that "this, too, shall pass."

Leafing through pages of my old journals provides valuable lessons for me that prove my tenacity and ability to bounce back from things that I thought would surely kill or destroy me. My journals bear witness to my life. Journaling has allowed me to dissect complicated problems and identify patterns that have been destructive to my growth. It has allowed me to be honest about what I'm feeling. Even while writing this book, I turned to journal entries to see what things I struggled with, and I used my journal as a resource to be able to write authentically about issues that I had dealt with in the past. Journaling can also help with anxiety and stress. Thus, I believe every Black woman should buy herself a beautiful journal and begin writing right away. Make sure you find a good hiding place for it and don't forget where you hid it, which has happened to me far too many times! That memory ain't what it used to be!

MASSAGE

I love physical touch, but I have never been quite comfortable asking for touch without thinking that it should be sexual. Looking back at my twenties and thirties, I now realize I had sexual encounters when what I actually wanted was to be physically touched, but I didn't know how to voice that. When I was getting regular massages, I finally made the connection that physical contact and touch did not always have to be about sex. Booking regular massages has been my saving grace. Now that I'm single, I realize how much I desire physical contact, hands on my body that feel kind, soft, and pleasing. I used to view massage as indulgent or something for special occasions.

However, I now book monthly two-hour massages. Yes, two hours! Why? Because I'm worth it.

My grandmother was 81 years old and dying of terminal cancer when she finally agreed to get a massage. It was life-transforming for my grandmother, who questioned why she had never done this before. She was a woman who seemed to carry the world on her back but did not think she was worthy of having someone laying hands on her. Whenever my mother comes to town, I book her a two-hour massage. I want her to know she is worthy and deserving of this experience. My mother promptly falls asleep on the massage table, but she loves it. I'm glad I introduced this practice to my mother to help her relieve her stress.

I can't tell you how many of my clients are surprised to realize that their health insurance may cover massage. Look into that option as well. You deserve it!

DELEGATE

I have been self-employed for nearly 15 years, and I resisted hiring anyone. I'm Jamaican, and we all know the stereotype about us having 57 jobs. So I would be writing scripts, giving speeches, coaching clients, booking rehearsal rooms, teaching workshops, writing blogs, directing plays, sending invoices, scheduling meetings, cleaning my house, cooking, taking the car to the car wash, and mailing out the lifestyle planner I created! You name it, I would do it. Working 12 to 14 hours was the norm for me.

It wasn't until I read *The 4-Hour Workweek* by Timothy Ferriss that something shifted in me. And no, I never got my workweek down to four hours, but I did sit with the takeaway that I needed to delegate and shift my focus to doing the things that could only be done by me. I also had a Jamaican friend who bluntly said to me, "Trey, you need to stop running your business like a patty shop! (Also known as a mom-and-pop shop.) You are building an empire; you need to act like it. Hire people. At your level, you should not be creating and sending invoices!" I got defensive. I told her I enjoyed being hands-on with my business. But I knew she was right. I was a control freak, and by being so controlling, I was preventing the growth of my business. So, I got a notebook and wrote down all the things that could only be done by me. Then, I wrote down the things that I loved to do. I hired an assistant for the rest, which wasn't easy for me. I had to learn to let her do her job and stop micromanaging. I also hired a housekeeper who came in once per week to clean my home. Of course, I heard snide remarks from family members: "It must be nice . . ." A Facebook post by a friend who is a Black professor and a solo parent shared that she hired a housekeeper and that she felt guilty about having a woman of color cleaning her home. She also shared that she cleaned up her home before the housekeeper got there because she didn't want her to work too hard. And I totally related to her post. When I hired my housekeeper, I also struggled about who to hire. Eventually I opted to hire a woman of color because I wanted to ensure that my money was being circulated in the community.

Hiring a housekeeper and an assistant was a game changer for me. It gave me time to focus on my business and my dream. Once my son was born, I had the fantasy that I would be a working stay-at-home momma. I would strap my son to my chest and "wear" him as I typed away at my computer. How hard could it be? But my son had other plans for his tiny life, such as crying, eating, pooping, wanting to be held at all times, and never going to sleep. Two months in and with no traction on writing my book, I knew I had to hire someone. I eventually hired a full-time nanny who came in six days per week, cooked, did laundry, and watched my son. It wasn't an easy choice for me financially. My household had suddenly gone from two incomes to one. It was also right in the middle of the coronavirus pandemic, and my shows and talks were being canceled, which meant I was losing valuable income that I had been counting on. But I knew I needed the help. So I made some drastic cuts in my budget to afford the help that I needed.

So, take a look at your life. Are there things you need to delegate? Do you need to hire some folks to make your life easier? And yes, the reality of having the money to do so can be real, but, sis, please take a look at your expenses before ruling it out. Look at your lifestyle and see if there are some things you can cut to make this work. Sis, it's time you get the support you need.

ME TIME!

Emily Mills, from How She Hustles, is Black girl magic personified. She's a smart, daring creative entrepreneur who is building an empire that connects women all over the world. She is also the mother of two young boys. She shared that once per month, she books herself into a hotel close to home while her husband watches over the kids. As an entrepreneur and mother, she said she needed to trust that her husband was capable of looking after the kids so that she did not have to feel guilty about needing this time.

"Me time" is so important. You are a better mother, partner, and boss if you take some time for yourself. I once had a client who had a very stressful job, and she said upon arriving home, her partner and kids would just bombard her. She began to feel resentful and overwhelmed. I instructed her to inform her partner and her kids that when she got home, she needed 15 minutes to decompress. So upon arriving home, she wouldn't say a word to anyone, and she would head straight to the balcony and smoke a cigar. This was her way of taking time for herself before jumping into mommy duties. It worked for her family, and they were respectful enough to grant her that time because they saw that when she didn't take it, she was stressed out and cranky. So maybe you can't take a weekend once per month, but can you find 15 minutes in your day that belongs just to you?

GIRLFRIEND TIME

Every Friday, a few of my closest friends and I link up for happy hour at a local bar. Since becoming a new mom, I can't go every Friday, but I do try to make as many of these get-togethers as possible. It's important for me to have this girlfriend time and just be myself and not just someone's mom. Girlfriend time is important. Due to social media, many of us have this false sense of connection, and we think we are up to date on our friends' lives. However, we need to be intentional with our friends. Nurturing those connections is so important.

WHITE SPACE IN YOUR CALENDAR

Can I tell you a secret? I used to love looking at my full calendar. It made me feel important to have every single minute booked. I would squeeze in meetings whenever I could and would add more and more things to show myself and the world how productive I was. As I became more mindful of my energy and how I spent my time, I began taking things off my calendar, and this made a huge difference. By not multi-tasking numerous things throughout my day, I was able to be more focused. I was less stressed because I wasn't running from one meeting to another. I made time to have lunch with my son, which helped with our bonding. Taking time away from my work actually gave me more energy throughout the day instead of feeling totally drained when I pushed myself to work non-stop. Being deliberate about scheduling breaks in my day that sometimes include an afternoon meditation or a quick 15-minute walk outside to clear my head truly helped me to be more productive.

Sis, take it from me: be deliberate and conscious about your time instead of adding to your jam-packed calendar. Take a look at that bad boy and see what you can take off. One of my clients and her husband both worked full-time and had two kids, ages 7 and 10. My client spent most of her evenings taking her kids to soccer practices and swimming lessons. The weekend was also jammed packed with karate, basketball, and birthday parties. She felt exhausted and as though she and her husband were two ships passing in the night. When I suggested creating a white space in her calendar where she wouldn't book anything, she looked at me as if I were crazy. I advised her that effective immediately, the kids were allowed to pick one activity each. And from now on, the family would practice what

I termed "lazy Sundays," where they were not allowed to leave the house and had to do nothing but stay in their pajamas all day, watch movies, and play board games. They also had to unplug from all devices until 3 P.M. on Sunday. At first, her family resisted, but they eventually got on board. A few months later, she reported that the kids loved it. Her daughter also expressed that she was tired of always going somewhere. Her introverted son was getting better marks in school and expressed to his parents that he felt pressured to always be good at everything; now he just enjoyed hanging out with them. My client and husband now enjoyed cooking breakfast together in their pj's. She felt she was more present as a wife and less frazzled as a parent. She also schedules a bath for herself on Sundays now that she has the time to truly enjoy it.

As a society, we have fallen in love with being busy. Busy shows we are successful, and we are getting shit done! I used to wear my busy badge with honor. It made me feel good. I also was raised by women who would eagerly quote, "The devil finds work for idle hands." To appear to be resting or doing nothing was frowned upon. So it makes sense that the thing I struggle with the most is doing nothing. But creating white space in your calendar is a good thing for your mental health. It gives you time to do things such as take a long bath, read a book, garden, or take a walk and just spend valuable time with your loved ones.

FIND YOUR FUN

We have forgotten how to have fun. When I was a little girl, I loved riding my bike, playing hopscotch, battling it out in a game of Monopoly or roller skating at high speed down a hill. But as I grew older that fun little Black girl disappeared.

A few years ago, while filling out a form for the adoption process, there were some questions that asked, "What do you do for fun? What are your hobbies?" I was stumped. Fun? Apparently, people were out there having fun? Who knew! I racked my brain for the fun activities I participated in. I actually could not think of a thing. Because I loved my work, most of my time and energy revolved around that. Even when I went out, it was usually to some sort of industry function. In my downtime, I spent countless hours reading about the industry, and even a night at home involved watching TV shows and dissecting the plot to see what the writer could have done differently. It was pathetic to admit, but I didn't really have any fun. I knew this had to change, so I actually wrote a Facebook post asking folks what they did for fun. I was surprised when people suggested going to an amusement park, mini-golfing, roller skating, and organizing a game night. I googled my local roller-skating rink and called my friends, and we all went to an old school night of roller skating. It was amazing! So much damn fun! I also now try to go to an amusement park during the summer holidays. And I recently bought a pair of rollerblades. When I want quiet fun, I enjoy coloring or doing puzzles. Of course, now that I'm a mother, my fun time has slowed down somewhat; however, anytime I start to feel overwhelmed and drained, I know it's because I have stopped adding fun to my life and schedule. You need adult fun, so put that on your calendar!

THIS BLACK GIRL AIN'T GOT RHYTHM BUT SHE LOVES TO DANCE

In high school, I was in a pop group. I'm not a great singer, but my grandmother was my personal hype woman, so she told me to just go for it! I gave most of the major singing parts to the other members, and I wrote all the song lyrics and also rapped. I was really good at that, and I would rewind my cassette tape of *Ladies First* by Queen Latifah, dreaming of the day that the Queen would invite me on tour with her. I wanted to be the next Queen Latifah, so I went into the studio and put my magical lyrics down on plastic. I was so excited about the release of my CD, but only my grandmother bought it, and that was the end of my music career! But that dream has never died. I still have dreams of being on stage, rapping with the Queen, and my love of music still remains. Every time I find myself going into a slump, I pop on my favorite song and sing along. I'm also a die-hard hip-hop fan! Give me some Biggie and Drake (shout out to 'da 6!), and all of a sudden, I feel invincible.

I also love to dance! And the stereotype that all Black people can dance, well . . . if you see me dancing you will know for sure that it's indeed a stereotype. My friends tell me that I seem to be hearing something different from everybody else. And I didn't believe them until one day I watched a video of me dancing at a friend's birthday party. I was shocked. Who was this girl who moved as if she needed an exorcism? I didn't have a drop of rhythm! I made Oprah look like she was Ciara on the dance floor. And, girl, I love me some Oprah, but we all know she can't dance either. And watching myself, I wondered if Oprah also knew she couldn't dance? I watched in horror at my inability to catch the beat—I seemed to be at least a couple

of seconds behind the bass. And then I burst into hysterical laughter. I was a hot mess on the dance floor, but I was
having so much fun! So I didn't let the realization that I
would never be a backup dancer for Janet or Beyoncé stop
me. But I did decide to calm it down a little bit and forgo
the new TikTok dance craze and just stick to some moves
that I thought I had mastered.

And at all my live shows, I come out dancing on stage
to the glee of my audience. They cheer me along, so I get
even more hyped. And I think they think if Trey can do
all that dance nonsense without a care, why not me? And
when I'm at home, I always dance like no one is watching.
Music and dancing have been my go-tos to cheer myself
up. So, if you want to be a Black girl in love with yourself,
create your favorite, "Yes, I'm That Bitch" playlist! And,
sis, play it often so you don't forget who the hell you are!
Sometimes you gotta remind them! But sometimes you
gotta remind your damn self!

SIS, GET YOUR MIND RIGHT!

1. At work, do you have a support person/
    confidant whom you can trust? If not, who
    can you access outside of work to be that
    support person?

2. In your journal, on a scale of 1 to 10, rate how
    well you take care of yourself, 1 being low
    and 10 being high.

3. Rate your emotional well-being. Are you
    experiencing any feelings of doom? Are you
    scared of being in social settings? Or are you
    feeling irritable? Tired? Emotional? How

long has this been going on? Do you suspect that you may be depressed or suffering from anxiety? If so, stop what you're doing right now and go book an appointment to see a therapist or psychiatrist.

4. Pick two of the self-help tips such as delegate, exercise, or fun. And for the next two months, commit to using them as you make necessary changes to your life to help you feel better.

5. Every day affirm, "I am worthy of giving myself time to rest and play."

affirmations

I AM WORTHY OF GIVING MYSELF TIME TO REST AND PLAY.

I AM WELL RESTED AND HAPPY.

WHEN NEEDED I SEEK THE HELP OF OTHERS, AND THEY ARE ALWAYS HAPPY TO ASSIST ME.

chapter 8

Getting Rid of 'da Drama in Your Life

BLACK GIRL PLAYLIST:
"NO MORE DRAMA,"
MARY J. BLIGE

It was in all the tabloids: Mary J. Blige had broken up with her husband/manager, and it was ugly. There were accusations that he had cheated and was demanding an outrageous amount of spousal support from her. A few days after the news broke, I went to see her in concert. I love Mary. Her songs have been the soundtrack to my life. And Mary did not disappoint; she was on fire! Mary sang her heart out. She fell to her knees, holding back tears as she sang each painful lyric. It was obvious to everyone that this was a woman who was not only singing about the deepest heartbreak, but she was also reliving the drama of it right before our eyes. Mary sucked me in. It was difficult to watch yet so compelling I couldn't take my eyes off her as she delved into her raw, animalistic pain. I was in tears; Mary and I were one. As she sang about each heartbreak, I reflected on every damn person who had done wrong by me in the love department. When I left the concert, I thought to myself, *If Mary J. Blige didn't have drama in her life, what would she sing about?* I realized that many of us are die-hard fans because we are hooked to the drama of Mary's life, and many of us live as if we are her backup singers!

Many of us create drama in our lives, claiming we don't like it, but it's what we know, and it's how we thrive! I've had many clients who have come to me confused about why they always find themselves in drama. And drama can show up in our lives in so many different ways—in our relationships, friendships, work, and families. So let's take a look at how we spin more drama than on *The Young and the Restless*.

DAMN, GIRL, YOU'VE GOT RELATIONSHIP DRAMA!

Do you have a clear blueprint of what a healthy relationship looks like? Who are your relationship role models? Do you tend to find yourself in relationship drama? Cheating, emotionally unavailable partners, physically or emotionally abusive relationships? Chances are that if you grew up in a chaotic environment, you will create that chaos in your adult life. At my live events, the question I get asked the most by women is, "Trey, how do I find Mr. Right? I keep picking losers. Different names. Same guy. Same drama."

Sounds familiar? My answer is pretty simple. *You* have to realize you are the common denominator in your relationship drama. Sis, by now, *you* need to be able to see the drama coming and say, "Not today, Satan," and cross the damn street! Don't entertain it. Don't say hi. Don't invite it into your house and definitely not into your bed! *You* need to start holding yourself accountable! *You* need to recognize that drama may come driving a nice car or with the most swag on the block and may have a dazzling white smile, is six foot three, and is packing 'da goods. And yes, some well-packed goods can make us do some crazy thangs! But all the same, it's still damn drama! You can put lipstick on a pig, but it's still a pig! And, sis, here's what we're not going to do: we are not going to ignore the red flags, that gut feeling that tells you something is wrong. You don't need proof; you've been here before. Trust that you know what you know; this ain't your first rodeo.

Choose something different. Go a different route. And yes, girl, change up your "type." Often I will tell my clients that just because a certain individual doesn't make you cream your panties the first time you meet them doesn't mean this isn't your person! Attraction can grow. You'll be surprised how qualities such as kindness, compassion, being a good conversationalist, trustworthiness, reliability, being family-oriented, and honesty can make someone more attractive. Give them a chance. I always say give it three dates before deciding whether to move on; you might just surprise yourself.

EVERYBODY UP IN YOUR GIRL'S BUSINESS DRAMA!

My grandmother used to say, "Trey, your left hand doesn't have to always know what the right hand is doing." In other words, not everyone needs to be in your mix. I learned that the hard way. I had a relationship that had the potential to be a very solid one. We had a lot in common, shared similar goals and values, sex was amazing, and we both shared the same love for hip-hop and urban comedy. It was a match made in heaven. Yet, whenever we had disagreements, instead of talking to each other, we would talk to our friends and family. My partner would receive advice from her crew, and I would receive advice from mine. There were a lot of people involved in our relationship, and sometimes, we would receive conflicting advice, which led to more arguments. In our friendship circle, we had taken on the role of the couple who would provide the drama for everyone. And folks were more than eager to take up the front row seats in our lives.

And if there is one lesson that I have learned, it is that people will counsel you from where *they* are, not from where you are and what may be right for you. So, for example, you may have concerns about your partner's drinking because it has become an issue, and one too many times, it has caused your partner to act irrationally. If you seek advice from a friend who is single and recently got hurt in a relationship, chances are your friend will caution you about "not taking any shit in your relationship" and will advise you, "Sis, walk away. Don't do it, girl. You can do better all by yourself! You don't need a damn alcoholic in your life!"

You can present the exact same scenario to someone who's in a long-term relationship but not necessarily happy, and their advice may be, "No one's perfect. Work it out. Relationships take a lot of work. Stick with it. Maybe you're overreacting because you're not a drinker, plus it's better than being single."

Each of your friends has given you valid advice, but who is wrong and who is right? Neither. Both are looking at your scenario from their own vantage point and not necessarily what's best for you. In my past relationship where we were gathering advice from all our friends and family, their advice added more to our confusion. We also got hooked on the drama of doing a public weigh-in on things that should have remained private. Sadly, the outcome was that we broke up, and upon reflection, I think we should have made it. But we gave too many people access to our lives, and their access created more drama instead of helping the situation. So be careful about seeking relationship advice from friends. Try to work things out among yourself first, and if the problem persists, seek a professional therapist, relationship coach, counselor, or pastor/spiritual guide. Whatever you do, don't turn your relationship into a drama to entertain your friends!

CUBICLE CANISHA DRAMA

Be honest: Are you spending way too much time at the water cooler? Or are you the person who likes to gossip about your co-worker and ignite work drama instead of diffusing it? Are you a mean girl at work? And do you like to pit your co-workers against each other? Do you have a co-worker that you hate and don't talk to? Or do you fire off a fiery e-mail instead of thinking it through?

We spend a lot of time at work, so it can be a place where we are tempted to create some drama so things don't feel as mundane. But, girl, you know you are better than that. Make work the place where you are there to get the job done and go home. Don't get caught up in the office politics when co-workers try to drag you into it; be clear that you ain't the one! Often, being a Black woman at work is stressful enough, and because so many times things chip away at us, we are already on the defensive, even when we don't have to be. Recently, I sent what I thought was a simple inquiry e-mail to another work acquaintance who is a Black woman working in a highly stressful environment. Her response to my inquiry was met with defensiveness and blatant rudeness. I was so taken aback by her response that I was tempted to take my earrings off, put on some Vaseline, and go head to head with her. But I paused before hitting Send on my snarky response, and I chose to start all over again. Why? Because I did not want to start drama in my work environment.

And I also tried to offer her some compassion. I thought about who she is, another Black woman at the top of her game in an industry that is always questioning her ability and why she needed to be there. I knew she felt safe taking her frustrations out on me because I was another Black woman. And even though she was wrong for that, I understood it because I had been her many times in the past, taking out my frustrations on people who were trying to support me. I immediately felt empathy for her. It was obvious this was a hurt sister. She was hurt by someone else and could only respond to me by being hurtful herself. So I simply wrote back. "I'm sorry if you misconstrued my e-mail. My intent was to ask a simple question, not to question your ability. I truly try my best to walk through this world, creating as little harm to Black women as possible. So if my inquiry hurt or harmed you in any way, I'm sorry."

I would love to say she then wrote me back an apology and we met up and oiled each other's scalps and all was well in our Wakanda Sister Power Movement. But no, she didn't even respond. But that was enough for me. My mission was to diffuse drama in my work life. I didn't desire for her to drag me into what was going on with her, and obviously, from her response, I knew that something was going on with her. And that night, I held her at the top of my prayer list and just prayed she would feel love and support wherever she went.

We need to be clear that we will not engage in work drama; it is not good for our mental well-being or professional advancement. Whenever folks try to drag you into work drama, have a clear and ready response. For example, your co-worker, Cubicle Canisha, slithers out of her cubicle and heads straight toward you and says, "Girl, did you hear that Janice was given a promotion? It's obvious that Laurie was more qualified! Girl, what type of nonsense is that?"

You respond, "Sorry, girl, I've got to finish this report by five P.M!" and then immediately start furiously typing away at your computer. She will get the hint, especially if you do this every time her gossipy ass shows up at your desk! The only way drama can enter your life is if you continue to entertain it. And as tempting as it is, don't do it.

DYSFUNCTIONAL FAMILY DRAMA

My brother is the middle child of the family. Sandwiched between me, the oldest, and our baby sister. He's the only boy, and I used to think that is why he tends to be very level-headed and resists getting dragged into our family drama. My mother, grandmother, sister, and I would talk several times per day about everything that was going on in our extended family. Who wasn't talking to whom, who owed someone money, whose baby mama just slashed his tires, who has cancer, and who's definitely way too big to be wearing that dress at Auntie Pearl's wedding. Whenever we tried to engage my brother, he wasn't having it. He would politely change the subject or just not answer the phone. He had very clear guidelines that he enforced about how he would participate in our family. Every Sunday, he would call each of us individually and have a pleasant conversation on FaceTime. No regular group chats for him. If he was in a really good mood, sometimes he would agree to a three-way conversation. If you made plans to visit his home, he would firmly and politely put in a three-day visit restriction. No one could possibly overextend their welcome.

We really thought he had gone too far when his wife was pregnant with their first child and he put down some hard rules with the family. A few weeks before the birth, my mother just assumed that her presence would be needed, so she had her bags packed and waiting at the door, on standby for the birth of her grandson. So you can imagine how shocked we were when my brother informed my mother that he didn't want her there; he didn't want to stress out his wife, and he and his wife wanted some uninterrupted family time to bond with their new son. The "no invite" was also extended to my sister and me, and he told us that when they were ready to have visitors, they would let us know! We were outraged, and my mother was hurt, but my brother was unfazed. He stood his ground, and we just had to deal with it as my brother continued to live his best damn life. Soon he and my mother made up, and all was forgiven, but everyone was clear that my brother meant what he said and said what he meant. And sometimes that meant that your feelings were going to get hurt.

I, however, found his so-called boundaries to be unreasonable and selfish! So I reported him to my therapist! I was shocked by her response. She said, "Your brother is the only one in your family who knows how to set boundaries.

And that is why you're upset with him. You want to be him, but you're scared that if you start making your needs a priority and start taking care of your needs, your family will view you as selfish."

I knew she was right because I immediately got defensive and tried to list more ways that I found him selfish. My therapist would not be swayed. She didn't agree. I went home and thought about what she said. She was right— my brother was the most functional person in our family. He didn't have this codependency relationship with our mother like my sister and I had. He didn't create drama, and he didn't engage in it. I knew there was a lesson to be learned. I needed to stop the family drama in my own life. Slowly and carefully, I started to detangle from my grandmother, mother, and sister. I reduced our phone calls, and when they were bickering among themselves, I no longer tried to play referee; I just made up an excuse to get off the phone. I implemented a firm visitation rule that three to four days was good enough. We no longer needed to have these extended vacations that usually ended up in a fight. Now we could see each other for short family fun, and I sometimes opted to stay in a hotel so I could choose to leave when I wanted to and when things got tense.

My mother was truly insulted by this, but I stood my ground. I chose to no longer engage in any sort of gossip about extended family, and whenever my grandmother tried to drag me into it, I told her I found it to be too negative. At first my grandmother was upset and tried to bamboozle me into conversations. But after several months of politely shutting it down, she would start the conversation with, "I'm not being negative, but . . ." I couldn't help but laugh. So now at least she could see she was being negative, and her behavior did change. She now knew that I wouldn't engage in family gossip.

The biggest change for me was that I stopped attending large family gatherings. Our large family gatherings were a hotbed for gossip, subtle put-downs, and competitions to see who had a better car, a bigger home, and whose children were more successful. I decided I didn't need to be there. In the past, I had attended because of obligation and wanting to appease my mother. Now I was no longer interested in engaging with folks whose children's names I couldn't quite remember and whose marriages I couldn't keep up with. I found that these gatherings tended to stress me out. I was always preparing myself for how to answer the question, "But, gyal, how you get so fat?"—a standard West Indian greeting. I was no longer willing to answer any other inappropriate question by an aging West Indian auntie.

When you start implementing firm boundaries, your family and loved ones will have a hard time respecting them, and you will be labeled as selfish or thinking you're better than everybody else. My mother was horrified by my decision, and I knew she thought it was a reflection of how she raised me. The feedback I heard through the family grapevine was that "she get money and switch!" Which was far from the truth. I just didn't want to engage with unhealthy family dynamics. But instead of looking within, it was easier for my family to place the blame on me. But I was very clear with my boundaries, and eventually, the invitations stopped because folks knew I wouldn't be coming. As I implemented these boundaries to avoid family drama, I found I actually started enjoying the deliberately planned time with my immediate family. We became closer as a family. I genuinely love my family, but like everything in your life, you need to create balance, you need to evaluate where you need to implement changes, and you need to be clear on what works for you and what doesn't. Make the necessary changes and stick with them, regardless of the fallout.

NOW EVERYBODY MAD: THE FALLOUT

When you start to create boundaries in your life, people will get upset. Actually, when you start to create boundaries in your life, people will get *damn* upset! No, this wasn't an editorial error. I needed to write it twice so you could understand that folks are gonna get mad. If you have been the go-to person in everyone's life, they are not going to deal with the changes well. Every family, every friendship, every relationship has a status quo when it comes to how things get done. There is a running order, and folks don't like it when you deviate from the order, especially if the order has been benefiting them. Usually, from the status quo/order, only one person or a limited few are benefiting from the "way things are done around here . . ." So when you make a conscious effort to make changes for sure, you will be met with resistance. Be prepared to be called selfish. Selfish is the word often thrown around when folks want to manipulate you or guilt you into doing things they want. Many of us have learned from our mothers and grandmothers that everyone's needs must come before your own. So when you start to put your own needs first, others will view it as selfish. They won't understand why you're not signing up for a lifetime of feeling underappreciated, exhausted, and unhappy. Misery does like company, and dysfunction loves dysfunction.

I remember when I was debating whether to end a long-term relationship, my grandmother questioned why I would want to end a relationship with someone who treated me reasonably well. I tried to explain. "Gran, I'm just not happy. I want more."

My grandmother looked at me with utter disbelief. "Oh, come on. Who's happy? No one's happy! We are all just getting by. Surviving! Your problem is you want too much."

I knew I didn't want to choose a life of survival. I knew I also wanted happiness. I deserved happiness in my life. I had to choose between happiness or survival, and the choice was obvious for me. I didn't want to be with someone with whom I had fallen out of love. I needed to say no to the expectations of my family and friends. Maybe they were okay with settling, but I wasn't.

NO! NOPE. NO WAY. NO, IT'S NOT POSSIBLE. NO. NO. NO.

Folks don't like the word no. And once you start saying a firm no, folks really start getting mad, especially if there isn't any explanation to follow it. "No" can be a complete sentence. I learned this lesson very eloquently in my twenties. There was an esteemed director who had been invited in to direct a workshop of my play. I was overjoyed. The other actors and I were in awe. During the rehearsal process, she was engaging and delightful, and I was learning so much from her. Lunchtime rolled around, and we were all getting ready to head out for lunch. I turned to her and asked, "Jennifer, would you like to join us for lunch?" She looked up from her script and said, "No."

I waited. I waited for her to offer a reason or at least an excuse, but she didn't. She just got up, popped her script in her bag, smiled, and breezed past us. I was shocked. For many years I sat with her clear example of no as a full sentence. I wanted to be her, and I tried to be that sort of woman who could just say no without an explanation. I always thought that once I hit 30, I would master it, but I didn't. And then I vowed that once I turned 40, I would be like Jennifer and just say no and breeze past anyone who had any damn questions. But I haven't gotten there yet. I'm still struggling with just saying no and feeling comfortable with that. But I am getting better at it, and my middle ground is now saying, "Unfortunately, that's not going to work for me" or "Unfortunately, I'm unable to do that."

I no longer offer an explanation, even though I can see by their shocked faces and wide-open mouths that they are waiting for one. But naw, girl, I'm too grown for that! Just know it ain't gonna work for me!

Yet when you start to say no more often and redesign your life to want more, many people will start to think, "Who do you think you are?" When they see you wanting more and actually getting more, it will make them take a hard look at their own lives, and sometimes it's easier for folks to bury their head in the sand than implement changes. Have you noticed among a group of friends who are all couples that when one couple breaks up, you can bet that within the next two years, most of the other couples will follow suit? For example, if Shannon and Paul, the "it couple" in the group, break up, often what happens is that folks start evaluating their own lives and relationships. And they start thinking, *If Shannon and Paul can break up, how come we're still hanging on? And why am I scared about leaving? Look at Shannon now! Yes, she went through a rough patch, but now she's thriving, she looks great, and she started a new relationship. It's obviously a better fit, and I've never seen her look happier!* Shannon interrupted the group dynamic and status quo and gave her friends permission to also make changes, and that is why the other couples start to eventually unravel.

Choosing to walk away from drama and changing the way things are done in your life and relationships will initially cause disruption with those close to you. But in the long run you will have more peace, happiness, and clear, firm boundaries that deflect drama. So don't give up. It may not be easy to make these changes, but it is necessary.

SIS, GET YOUR MIND RIGHT!

1. If you are currently in a relationship, rate it on a scale of 1–5, with 1 being Tina and Ike (We have no idea why we are still together and how to get out of this dysfunctional shit! I need out now!); 3 being Jada and Will (We know there's something worth fighting for. We've had a few "entanglements," but we are committed to working this shit out. I ain't going nowhere!); and 5 being Michelle and Barack (It doesn't get any better than this! Babe, I got you! I can't imagine anyone else by my side.)

2. How healthy is your relationship? How does drama show up in it? Who creates it and why?

3. Take a look at your past relationships and friendships and determine where drama showed up. Write down what you would do differently, if anything.

4. Assess your work environment. Do you add to the workplace drama? If so, how can you stop? If not, how can you continue to stay above the fray?

affirmations

MY LIFE IS PEACEFUL AND HAPPY.

I'M SO BLESSED TO HAVE HEALTHY
AND AMAZING RELATIONSHIPS.

I AM INTENTIONAL ABOUT CHOOSING RELATIONSHIPS
AND FRIENDSHIPS THAT ENCOURAGE MY GROWTH.

chapter 9

Sis, Make That Change

BLACK GIRL PLAYLIST:
"CHANGES I'VE BEEN GOING THROUGH,"
MARY J. BLIGE

I was on the phone with a friend who was trying to convince me to attend a party hosted by someone who I found obnoxious and draining on a good day. Yet this person was well connected and going to one of her events was definitely a sign that you had made it. Plus, I was at the point in my career that going to these sorts of things could really help me. Yet everything in my body screamed no. But I said yes, hung up the phone, and started getting ready. All fancy and party ready, I sighed as I got into the car and told myself I didn't even have to stay long—just circle the room and go home. But while backing out of my driveway, I saw myself in the mirror. I made eye contact with myself, and I knew I had changed my mind. This isn't how I wanted to spend my weekend. I was no longer interested in being around people that I didn't like. I no longer wanted to feel as if I was selling my soul and faking a smile because this person could possibly advance my career. Life is too short, and I wanted to spend my time with people I actually liked!

In my late twenties, I was engaged to my high school sweetheart. (Yes, I dated men!) We had been together for seven years. We had bought a house, and we were waiting for it to be built. Meanwhile we went to the builder's design center to pick out paint colors, floor tiles, and furniture. And three months before we closed, I called off the engagement. I had changed my mind. And yes, there was a lot of explaining to do, and my fiancé was hurt. I tried my best to be careful and respectful of his hurt while honoring my own journey, but I knew I had every right to change my mind even if it made no sense to anyone but me.

And, girl, I'm telling you, even if there is a mortgage involved, even if you're in your wedding dress, even if you got in the limo, you're at the altar, have two kids, have fancy letters behind your name, and you already said yes, you are allowed to change your damn mind! You are allowed to change the direction of your life at any given time. Be committed to change. Committed to changing your life, your surroundings, your mindset. I once wrote the following in my journal, and I read it often: "I changed, and that's okay. I started praying for me, betting on me. Manifesting and acting as if I could not fail. And with these simple changes came lost friends and loved ones who told me, 'You've changed!' And they were right. I had. And they made me realize that sometimes, to go to the next level, you have to lovingly and gently let go of who you used to be and those who want you to stay the same . . . Not everyone can come on your magical new journey, and sometimes you have to take action steps that prompt you to choose yourself. You choosing yourself is a scary thing, and some people won't like it and won't like the changes. But change anyway. Let them know you're changing, that you aren't even the Black girl you were yesterday!"

SIS, JUST BECAUSE YOUR MOMMA HAS PLASTIC ON HER FURNITURE DOESN'T MEAN YOU HAVE TO LIVE THAT!

Girl, I can bet you probably have a mother and grandmother who raised you to save all your good stuff. Good stuff could mean your socks, bedsheets, towels—even your damn panties! Come on, I know I ain't the only one with good panties saved away in my top drawer! But my grandmother took saving good things to a different level. My grandmother saved a whole damn room! Yes, we had an entire dining room that no one was allowed to go in. In that room, the couch and the chairs were covered with plastic that stuck to your legs and plush red velvet cushions were lined up in perfect order. My grandmother's favorite white porcelain figurines lined the shelves. And finally, a large color TV was the featured act in the room. It seemed to taunt us from its prominent place, begging us to break the rules and turn it on, but none of us would dare unless we wanted to get our ass whooped into the following week. My grandmother told us that she was saving the room for when "company" came over. So no one was allowed in that room unless we were going in there on Saturday afternoon with some furniture polish and a cloth to dust it. This became my job while my grandmother would give me the evil eye to ensure I put all her precious figurines back in their correct order. I would often fantasize about the day that company would come over and we could finally use the room and turn on the big TV, but our long-anticipated company never came.

I swore that when I grew up I would never have rooms in my home that no one was allowed to go in, but we are all creatures of our environment. Unlike Gran, I didn't save an entire damn room, but I did save good sheets, good pens, good socks, good running shoes to wear only if I had a show, and of course, I used my favorite perfume only on special occasions. I was so damn stingy to myself, that I didn't realize I was giving myself and the universe the underlying message that I was not worthy of good and nice things at all times. And I didn't trust those good things would last forever.

When my grandmother died and we went to pack up her home, I opened her favorite handcrafted wooden chest, and inside it was brand-new sheets, towels, hand towels, and pillowcases, most of them with the tags still on! I broke down crying because I thought she had worked so hard to buy these things, and she would not allow herself to enjoy them. She chose to use tattered, worn-out towels and sheets. She denied herself any form of goodness. She chose to save her best for a day that never came. My grandmother was a woman who chose to deny herself joy. Joy in big and small ways. I knew there was a lesson in all of this for me. I immediately went home and took my favorite towels out of my drawer and started using them. I put on my sexy new underwear, and I didn't give a damn that nobody was seeing them except me. I sprayed my favorite perfume, and to this day, I use my expensive favorite perfume every day, because I know I deserve to smell good. No more will I be a person who delays pleasure or joy. I live in the moment. Tomorrow isn't promised, so, girl, stop saving your good shit! Make a change today and start using it.

SIS, I AIN'T YOUR ENEMY. LET'S CHANGE HOW WE INTERACT WITH OTHER BLACK WOMEN.

"Why can't Black women get along? Why are we so mean to each other? I just smiled at another Black woman, and she gave me the stink eye?"

—A POST ON A FRIEND'S FACEBOOK PAGE

When I was little, my grandmother would often hiss into my ears, "Don't tell anyone your business because people will be jealous of you." Before heading out to visit family, my grandmother would also remind me that "anything that happens in my house stays in my house!" If we went over to my aunt's or any other family member's home, my grandmother would glare at me if she felt I was divulging too much of what she deemed her "business."

She also seemed to have a mistrust for most of the women in her life. As I got older and brought friends home, my grandmother would remind me again, "Not everyone is your friend. Be careful of so and so . . . she doesn't mean you any good; she's jealous of you." I don't know what had happened in my grandmother's life for her to come to this realization about all women, but I know what happened to me. I learned from my grandmother's own mistrust that no one could be trusted, especially other Black women. So, throughout my life, I walked around with a certain level of paranoia about other Black women, waiting for them to let me down at some point. Or spending most of my time trying to find and confirm the jealousy that I knew they harbored toward me. I also viewed them as competition and was very careful about what I shared with them. I was prepared at any given moment for a sistah to stab me in the back.

In my twenties, the Universe decided to test my theory. And it played itself out in full force. I had written my first play, *'Da Kink in My Hair*. I cast the play with several young Black women and a young Black female director. All of us were eager to make our mark in a world that had systematically ignored our existence. We were now audacious, fearless, Black women taking up space on stage and authentically telling our stories. Our small dream soon became bigger than we could even realize: we went from performing on the street corners of New York City to performing in sold-out 2,000-seat theaters and getting TV deals. Black women were flocking to hear our stories, and the play was a sold-out hit.

Here we were healing our community through our play, yet we were so fractured as a group behind the scenes. Apparently, they had also been given the same message in their homes: that we should not trust one another. Our mistrust of each other played out in destructive ways, and we did not have the coping skills or the maturity to deal with it without creating even more harm to one another. The play was dealing with heavy emotional issues such as suicide, incest, police brutality, and colorism. And all of us had shown up on this journey broken. We were young Black women doing the work, very important work under less-than-ideal circumstances. We were underpaid and overworked for most of the play's journey, and finally, when we started to get paid, we had arguments about who was making what and who was getting credit for what. Who had said what about someone behind their back and whose side we needed to be on. We tried our best to have constructive conversations, and we so desperately wanted to be that safe place for each other. But it led to more arguments, more hurt, and pain. Five years into the play's run and a successful television deal, we were worn out and were highly suspicious of one another. We were at a crossroads, and we were hurt, and we each chose to go our separate ways. My takeaway from that experience was my grandmother was right: Black women could not be trusted. I did not acknowledge that I had basically brought this experience into my life and manifested the outcome because I had walked into it with feelings of mistrust and betrayal geared at the entire team and the process. So the outcome was not a surprise.

It wasn't until I started to do my own inner healing work and began reading the popular Louise Hay book *You Can Heal Your Life* that I started to see how wrong my grandmother was. The book was a complete mind shift for me. It taught me that the world wasn't this unsafe place full of unhappy people who were eager to see me fail. People weren't sitting at home with a voodoo doll with my face on it, trying to cause me harm. And I'm not naive enough to believe that there isn't jealousy or envy in the world. We all know that bad-minded sistah who ain't happy for nobody! The one with the chip on her shoulder. The one who just always has that stank look on her face. The one who, if you ask her where she got her new fly shoes from, conveniently forgets where she bought them! (Girl, we see you, and we know who you are!) So we can leave her out of this equation. But I don't believe that every single person in the world is plotting your downfall. After doing more inner work and delving into the world of self-help, positive thinking, and being aware of the energy I was putting out to the world, I began to change my mindset. I make a conscious effort to celebrate Black women, trying to be a source of support for them instead of competition. Gabrielle Union also helped with this shift for me. I loved her Essence Black Women in Hollywood speech, where she eloquently shared that she used to be one of those women who would not celebrate other Black women, that Hollywood had pitted them against one another, and that growth and maturity had made her shift her view. And who could forget that moment that has now become the most popular Black girl meme—when Taraji Henson jumped out of her seat to congratulate Viola Davis. Her happiness was so palpable, it was as though she won. Or Miss Nigeria jumping up and down on the stage when Miss Jamaica won. This was the ultimate Black girl-power moment! Those are the images I now want to hold of Black women. This is who we are. So when one of us succeeds, I clap even harder. As my girl Issa Rae states, "I'm rooting for everybody Black!"

And it seems as if the Universe opened its arms to me the more I celebrated others. More opportunities came my way, and more Black women came to my aid. When I got my first book deal, I immediately got on the phone and called another Black woman, Elayne Fluker, who's the boss lady of the *Support Is Sexy* podcast. She had recently gotten a prominent book deal. I asked her some questions about her deal, and she not only shared how much she made on her deal and encouraged me to negotiate higher, but she offered to introduce me to her agent to help broker my deal. With her help, I was able to demystify the world of publishing, make more money, and educate myself. Later I passed on this knowledge to another sistah who called me about her own deal with another publishing house. We need to know that when one of us gets through the door, it's our responsibility to hold the door even wider for the other woman to walk through. There is enough to go around. We do not have to believe that played-out, damaging myth that Black women do not support one another. That is not true! I would not have the career and success I have today if it wasn't for Black women showing me mad love and support. Black women continue to support me and hold me down. So, let's change that narrative and start giving each other some love! Send some flowers, write a gushing Facebook post, send some resources and information to a Black woman that you admire. It's time that we start bigging each other up. (For my non-Jamaicans, that means it's time to start celebrating each other).

SIS, LET'S CHANGE YOU BEING SO HARD ON YOURSELF!

I'm in the public's eye. I produce theater, plays, movies, and TV shows, and put on several *Black Girl in Love (with Herself)* events that inspire thousands of women. My work, my ideas, and my thoughts are all out there for public consumption. So having a public platform leaves me wide open for lots of praise but also harsh criticism. And no matter how many people buy a ticket to my show or send me e-mail telling me how much my work has changed their life, I would often ignore that and zoom in on that one troll who had something negative to say. Their comment would keep me up at night, and I would spend time trying to reason with them on Facebook, trying to get them to change their mind, trying to get them to like me. The need to be liked was so strong for me that I would often write long, detailed e-mail messages to trolls, trying to figure out how I could change their offending opinions about me. I would not put the same amount of energy into responding to folks who told me they loved my work, or how much my work had changed their lives. And theater reviews were the worst. I would breeze past glowing reviews, but if a critic wrote that they hated my work or "didn't get it," I was wounded for weeks. A bad review would send me to bed, and I would feel humiliated.

In 2005, my play *'Da Kink in My Hair* was in Canada's most prominent theater, the Princess of Wales Theatre. It was the hottest ticket in the city. We were the toast of the town. Yet within the theater community, not everyone was happy. We were young Black girls redefining what theater could be, unapologetically taking up space in venues that were not meant for us. So, it wasn't surprising that there was a need to clip our Black girl wings and put us back in our place. And it was challenging dealing with bad reviews, but there was one particular review that was so vile and loaded it felt like a personal attack, as if the critic had a vendetta against me and wanted to publicly humiliate me. The review was written by a trusted critic for a popular newspaper. And his unflinching review was there for everyone to read. And the quote that stood out to me was "'*Da Kink* is the ghetto *Lion King.*" The reviewer then proceeded to bash me and the play, naming all the reasons why we were not deserving of the accolades and attention. I broke down crying in my dressing room. One of the actors rushed to me and ripped the page out of the newspaper. She then lit a stick of sage, and proceeded to burn it as she turned to me and said, "We don't do our work for them, we do it for Black women who need to see themselves . . . It was never meant for them, and that is why they are upset because they are so used to it always being about them. You must never forget who you are."

Something shifted in me then. I realized that the reviewers and the trolls had tapped into that little girl inside me who was extremely hard on herself, so she desperately wanted and needed everyone to love her. The little girl who always felt she had no right to be there. And I realized I did not have to please everyone. I didn't have to take their criticism or even my own. I was doing my best, and I needed to recognize that. I needed to stop being so critical of myself and stop allowing people's criticism of me to leave me so broken. I also needed to focus on the good and stop giving energy to the bad. So my advice to you, sis, is don't allow people to get inside your head. Don't allow them to chip away at your self-esteem. Don't let them steal your Black girl joy!

The more powerful you are, the more some folks will be invested in trying to steal your joy. They will try to get you. Society isn't used to Black women taking up space, and they will do their best to put you "back in your place." The most blatant example of this is how the media treated powerful Black women like Michelle Obama and Serena Williams. Women who were publicly in spaces never before occupied by Black women. And the attacks were brutal. From calling Mrs. Obama the President's baby mama to comparing both women to animals, the media's treatment of these women was relentless and shocking to witness. Many of us as Black women were all too familiar with this treatment, and to witness it on such a public stage had many of us collectively holding these women in prayer, praying they would not crack under pressure. The ambush of these women was done to chip away at their self-esteem, and I often wondered how they managed to get through it. I think it's because they obviously had a true sense of who they were and what they brought to the table and a true sense of their purpose. These women are true examples of remembering who the fuck you are! So, sis, always remember who you are. You ain't ice cream— not everyone is going to love you. So don't be so hard on yourself and don't let the criticism get inside your head. Tell them to take several seats while you have a Kanye West moment and declare daily how great you are!

SIS, CHANGE HOW YOU CELEBRATE YOUR WINS!

I'm a type A personality. An overachiever. I have a list. *The* list of goals outlining all the things I want to accomplish in my life. It is detailed with action steps. I also have a vision board that I look at every morning to ensure I keep on track. I thrive on holding myself accountable, and I know many of my accomplishments and successes are tied to my ability to keep focused on tasks and ticking them off my to-do list. But often, when I accomplish a goal and ticked it off my list, I immediately would be on to the next thing. I didn't take the time to celebrate my wins. I also didn't want to seem as if I were bragging, so I kept my good news to myself, or if folks tried to congratulate me, I would downplay my accomplishments and pretend it wasn't a big deal. But I started to lose my zest for life— nothing felt satisfying. Something felt like it was missing, and I wasn't sure what I was working toward anymore.

It occurred to me that I was feeling this way because I didn't celebrate my wins. I came from a family who didn't make a big deal of successes. If I got three A's on my report card, and one B, the focus was placed on the B, with them asking, "What is this B doing here?" Even now, with many of my accomplishments, my parents seldom tell me they are proud of me. Once in a while my mom will surprise me and write under a Facebook post that she is proud of me. And it secretly makes my day! Yet what I find funny is that, often, when I meet my parents' friends, they will list all my accomplishments and relay to me how proud my parents are. I was surprised to learn that my father had a WhatsApp group where he was forwarding all my newspaper clippings and interviews to his friends and family while never saying a word to me! So because no one seemed to celebrate or acknowledge my success or wins, I didn't allow myself to dwell even for a minute on my success. I knew that had to change because deep within me there seemed to be this empty hole that needed to be filled. I needed validation. I wanted to be seen. Patted on the back. I wanted to confirm to myself that my hard work was paying off, and it was indeed something that needed to be celebrated.

I now celebrate all my wins, big and small. If I meet my writing goal for the week, I literally give myself a gold star in my journal. It may sound silly, but I like seeing gold stickers in my journals. It's a reminder to me that I did my best and accomplished a goal. For bigger wins, I now take myself out to dinner and sometimes invite loved ones out to celebrate with me. I don't immediately go on to the next thing on my list; I intentionally take a few days to bask in my accomplishment, and I write in my journal about how I feel about accomplishing my goal. Also, I do mirror work. I look into my eyes and say the words that I wanted and desired my parents to say: "Trey, I'm proud of you. Good job. You worked hard. You are deserving of this success." I acknowledge to myself that I have accomplished historical things, such as being the first Black woman in Canada to have her own TV show. I have created history, and I need to recognize that I did this, and it needs to be celebrated.

And I encourage my friends to do the same. A friend recently sent me an e-mail and was giving me a few updates on her life, and casually, at the end of her e-mail, she mentioned that she had been promoted. She was now running an entire damn department with a huge budget. She then went on to mention some other whimsical things, which I knew she was adding to downplay her accomplishments. I immediately called her and said, "Girl, stop that damn shit! We are going out to celebrate. This is a huge deal. You're a big fucking deal!" She was bashful at first, but then I became her personal hype woman. We got so excited on the phone that soon she was dying of laughter and yelling, "I'm a big fucking deal." And that night, we went out and celebrated. I kept telling her how proud I was. And I could see that little girl in her who needed to hear that. We need to celebrate not only our wins but our friends' wins. Don't allow your friends to play small, and don't allow yourself to do it either! I recently started a Friday shout out on my IG page @blackgirlinlove where I encourage women to share their weekly big and small wins. I call it the "Friday Gyal, Big Up Yourself!" I want women to know that it's okay to brag about yourself. You must celebrate all your wins! Yes, girl, celebrate you every day!

SIS, STOP HOLDING ON TO BLACK GIRL SHAME!

I was in huge despair as the deadline for my book approached. I had a few months to finish writing the book and turn it in to the editor. Meanwhile, I was dealing with an upcoming move, a devastating breakup, a newborn, and finalizing an adoption and going back and forth with lawyers. I also had two live shows I was producing and a workshop. One of these things by itself would cause major disruption or stress to a person's life. I was dealing with all of these things at the same time. I was beyond stressed, and I wasn't eating or sleeping. I was in a haze, barely being able to string a sentence together much less write a book. I had hit rock bottom but didn't realize my rock bottom also had steps that led to a furnished basement suite below! It was a deluxe rock bottom that was threatening to put me in the grave.

After tossing and turning while trying to figure out how I was going to handle the various demands on my life, I leaped out of bed. It was 3:47 A.M., and I frantically dialed my good friend's number. Thank God she answered because I was truly at my lowest and I was hysterical. She tried her best to calm me down, and she put me on speakerphone as she and her wife took turns trying to make sense of my ramblings. I ran through my list of all the things I needed to do, barely catching my breath, hyperventilating through my tears. My friend's wife—a brilliant, smart lawyer—took control of the situation. She calmly told me to get a piece of paper and methodically went through everything that I needed to do, what things required my immediate attention, what things I could completely take off my plate, and what things could be done at a later date.

When she suggested I call my editor and ask for an extension, I immediately shot it down. How could I? Here I was, this little Black girl who was given this opportunity by the largest self-help publishing house in North America to write a book and I was going to call them and tell them that I couldn't do it! I thought of how many Black women were dying to be in my shoes and of how it would look if I didn't rise gloriously to the occasion. I would be letting down my race and letting down every other Black woman who might possibly be considered to write for them in the near future. They would now be viewed as lazy, undisciplined, and unprofessional. I shared my fears with my friend, and she immediately called it unnecessary "Black girl shame." Shame that was unwarranted. She assured me I was not undisciplined or unprofessional and that I was actually the opposite and the book deal was an example of my hard work. There was no need for me to carry the entire race on my back. What was needed was for me to recognize that I was burned out, dealing with numerous traumas, and I had too much on my plate. Instead of feeling shameful, I needed to offer myself compassion and understanding. I knew she was right, and through my sobs, I agreed.

I got off the phone and started to compose an e-mail to my editor, explaining why I would be unable to meet the deadline. I also clearly named my Black girl shame. I told her about the ironies of writing a book about Black women living balanced and better lives, and here I was feeling overworked and stressed, carrying unnecessary shame and guilt. And at that very moment, I was far from a Black girl in love (with herself). I hesitated and thought about revising the e-mail and sending something less personal and vulnerable, but I took a deep breath and hit Send. The rest of the night, I tried unsuccessfully to quiet the voices in my head that were convinced they would take away my book deal or fire me. The next morning, my editor responded with such grace and thoughtfulness. She immediately sympathized with me and commended me for sharing my feelings, and we went back and forth on various dates that would work for me to turn in the book, finally agreeing on a date that would give me an additional six weeks. I was so relieved and so grateful.

I realized then that throughout my life, various versions of Black girl shame had contributed to me pushing myself beyond my limits, saying yes to things that I didn't want to, ignoring the warning signs in my body that I was working too hard. When I shared this experience with some friends and engaged them about their own Black girl shame, one expressed that she never leaves the office earlier than any of her white co-workers because she carries the Black girl shame of them thinking that she is lazy or not working hard enough. She envied how white women are able to leave early or make mistakes at work and not think that it's a reflection on their entire race. In the article, "White Privilege: Unpacking the Invisible Knapsack," white feminist, anti-racism advocate Peggy McIntosh discusses all the ways in which white people benefit from their race and do not carry the burden of thinking that their individual behavior will be a reflection of their entire race. She writes, "I can be late to a meeting without having the lateness reflect on my race."

I have had to remind myself that I can have bad days and moments, and it's not a reflection of my race. I also have to give grace to other Black people and excuse them for having bad days. This happened recently while I was sitting in a business meeting. The company that was delivering the presentation, a Black start-up company led by three handsome brothers, had some technical difficulties with their presentation. I started to feel the shame rise, thinking, *Oh damn, they are going to make us all look bad* . . . But I swallowed my Black girl shame and cracked a joke, making a reference to a meeting that happened last month when a white team's laptop started to smoke and cause a small fire during the presentation. I boiled it down to shit sometimes happens! As everyone laughed, I could sense the relief of the presenting team and how grateful they were, because they knew I understood how stressful it can be being in a room full of white people and things not going according to plan. I gave them a reassuring smile, which I hoped conveyed to them that, brotha, I got you!

Black girl shame can happen in some really comical and subtle ways, and sometimes we have to laugh at the absurdity of it all. I recall working with a client who came to me stressed about her job and the extra pressure of being in charge of an intern who was, as she explained, "determined to make her look bad." The intern, a young Black woman, would bring fried chicken to work and eat it in the lunchroom, and my client felt this was not professional. Gently prodding, I asked her if this intern were white, if she would care if she ate fried chicken. My client, of course, said she wouldn't, but that wasn't the point. I raised my eyebrow and gave her one of my "Girl, stop your damn nonsense" looks. We then went into a lively and humorous discussion about Black girl shame and how it shows up in our lives and how we need to name it and drop it. We do not need to carry the burden of being responsible for our entire race. It is stressful enough to be a Black woman; we do not have to carry shame that isn't ours. So whenever you are experiencing shame, take a deeper look and see if it's warranted, and if it isn't, change it!

SIS, GET YOUR MIND RIGHT!

1. Commit to doing mirror work for the next 90 days. Every morning, look yourself in the mirror and say, "_____, I'm so proud of you. I love you. You have worked so hard and deserve all your success."

2. Commit to picking one friend from your social media list every Friday and write some encouraging words on their page, expressing how proud you are of them. Let them know

that you see them and tell them what a good job they are doing. And if they are a small business owner, shout out their page on your own social media accounts. Give them a call to let them know you're proud of them.

3. In your journal, write about how Black girl shame has shown up in your life and how you can address further potential shame in your daily life.

affirmations

THE BIGGEST LOVE I CAN GIVE, I GIVE TO MYSELF.

I EMBRACE CHANGES IN MY LIFE, AND I ACCEPT ALL THINGS WITH GRACE AND EASE.

I CELEBRATE ALL MY FRIENDS WINS AND SUCCESSES AND THEY INSPIRE ME EVERY DAY TO BE BETTER!

chapter 10

Mindset, Manifestation, and Vision

BLACK GIRL PLAYLIST:
"HIGHER GROUND,"
SHAMEKA DWIGHT

My grandmother used to say, "Trey, you're born with luck. You will always be lucky because you were born with two gray hairs!" And yes, this indeed was the truth: as a baby, buried within my kinky coils were two gray hairs. My grandmother swore that meant God had marked me as his angel to perform good deeds. My grandmother promptly nicknamed me "Special." So I grew up believing that good things were supposed to happen to me, and I never doubted that. I walked through the world with this expectation. I would often feel sorry for the folks who didn't have the good fortune of having gray hair to protect them from bad luck. As I got older, I started to think that maybe it wasn't really luck but that perhaps my grandmother was just superstitious. But what was evident is my grandmother told me at a young age to expect to be lucky, so essentially, she set up my mindset to think that only good things could happen to me. And because I believed that, they did!

In my twenties, I didn't quite have the language or the insight to fully understand that what you think about will show up in your life. That you attract what you believe. So, I still thought I was lucky, but I wasn't intentional with my thoughts. But there was an inner understanding that something spiritual was at play because thoughts and wishes that I said aloud or thought about would come to pass. Often my friends would tease that it seemed as if I had a horseshoe up my ass or a direct pipeline to God. I didn't see it quite like that. However, it wasn't unusual for me to have daily conversations with God/Universe. In these conversations I would ask for direction and guidance to keep me on the chosen path that God intended for me.

Before the success of my play and TV show, I was a young counselor working in a shelter for abused women and children. I knew I wanted to be an actor, and I loved writing, but I had no idea how to create a fruitful living in the arts. One day, while walking down the street with a friend, we passed the Princess of Wales Theatre, Canada's largest commercial theater, and they were advertising *The Lion King*. I looked up at the marquee and said to my friend, "One of these days, my play is going to be at this theater." Bear in mind I had never written a play and had never acted before. My friend could barely contain her laughter and shot me a doubtful look. And I could understand her skepticism. I was a young Black girl from the projects who had never written anything, stating I was going to have a play at one of the most prominent theaters in Canada! Yet I held on to that belief, and for years, every time I walked by the theater, I would say, "I'm going to be here." I would write in my journal, "My play will be at the Princess of Wales Theatre."

Six years later, I wrote a play that I entered into the Fringe Festival, and overnight, it became a hit. I eventually got a call, and it was a producer from Mirvish Productions, the owners of the Princess of Wales Theatre. They wanted to meet. At the meeting, they expressed that they wanted to put my play on in the Royal Alexandra Theatre, a smaller theater that is right down the street from the Princess of Wales. I was happy but somewhat disappointed it wasn't the theater I had dreamed about. Boldly I asked, "Are you sure it shouldn't be at the Princess of Wales Theatre?" The producer nearly choked on his water. He was quite sure they had never had a Canadian show at the Princess of Wales Theatre; that theater only did big mainstream American productions. And I could tell the thing he didn't say was, "And you think your little Black show needs to be there?" I left the meeting thinking that perhaps I was wrong, and I should just be happy my play was now being commercially produced. But I couldn't let go of my dream and the nagging feeling they were the ones that had gotten it all wrong. My play deserved to be in the Princess of Wales Theatre. We began rehearsals a month before our show was supposed to open. Then the unexpected happened—negotiations for the big-budget, commercial show that was supposed to go into the Princess of Wales Theatre had fallen through, and the theater was now empty, and they needed a show! '*Da Kink* was going to open at the Princess of Wales Theatre. I could barely contain my excitement. I silently thanked the Universe, knowing that years ago, I declared it to the Universe, and it had listened to me and made it happen!

One quote I love so much—and I have debated having it tattooed on my body but I'm too much of a chicken—is a quote by Paulo Coelho from his book *The Alchemist*. It's a quote I read daily and recite every time I want to manifest something in my life.

"And, when you want something, all the universe conspires in helping you to achieve it."

But I will caution you. Be very specific about what you ask the Universe.

Anyone who knows me knows that my lifelong dream was to meet Oprah. When I was a 12-year-old girl holding down my household while my mother was at work, Oprah became the substitute mom for this little latchkey kid. I would get home from school at 3:30 P.M. every day, make myself and my brother a snack, and plop myself in front of the TV at 4 P.M. I was in awe to see a dark-skinned, chubby Black woman on TV. A woman who looked like me. Oprah gave me the hope that it was indeed possible to be on TV! And I knew that we were kindred spirits. She was also raised by her grandmother, she was an Aquarius like me, she loved reading, she loved *The Color Purple*, she struggled with her weight like me . . . The list was endless. I just knew Oprah was my mother in another lifetime. So I began a quest to meet her. Each week I would write a letter and pop it into a fluorescent envelope. My thinking was it would make it stand out from all the mail she got. But alas, after two years of letter writing and no luck, I gave up. Even my grandmother weighed in. "Bwoy, Oprah is really hard on you . . . I thought by now she would answer!" But despite not being successful at getting her attention, I still believed that we would meet one day.

So I was now in my thirties, and I heard that Oprah was coming to Toronto to screen her movie *Precious* at the Toronto Film Festival. I knew this was my moment. I knew I had to meet her. I started writing out my affirmation: "I'm so excited to meet Oprah." I wrote this in my journal every day for 90 days, writing it in clusters of groups of seven, because seven is my lucky number. I also visualized every day about meeting Oprah, what that would feel like. Of course, my friends and family did not hold out much hope. But I did. A friend and I purchased tickets for the screening. I carefully selected my outfit and I put on two pairs of Spanx because I wanted to ensure that I looked my best and as slim as possible when I finally met my idol.

At the screening, Oprah was on stage introducing the movie, and I was with my friend in the nosebleed seats. I realized my chance of meeting her was slim to none. But I say a prayer to the Universe: "Universe, please let me meet Oprah!" Once the movie was on, Oprah was nowhere in sight. I felt myself losing hope, and I was also feeling that I was about to pass out. My two pairs of Spanx were threatening to cut off my circulation. I whispered to my friend that I needed to go to the bathroom. She encouraged me to wait because she knew I didn't want to miss the ending. But I couldn't wait. I was hot, sweaty, experiencing thigh rub, and my Spanx were now pinching my inner thigh. I was in pain. I got up to head to the bathroom. I saw the signs indicating there was a bathroom upstairs and one downstairs. I decided that I needed to always be symbolically moving up, so I took the steps that lead to the bathroom upstairs.

Once I got there, I headed to the bathroom stall, my Spanx squeezing the damn life out of me. As I started to take them off, thankful that I was still breathing, I heard the bathroom door open. I kept one pair on and exited the stall, knowing I should hurry so I could catch the end of the movie. I headed toward the sink, and standing right in front of me with her shoes in her hands was Oprah Winfrey! I nearly passed out. I couldn't believe it, yet I believed it! I manifested this! She casually said, "Hi, how are you? My feet are killing me!" I noticed she had her shoes in her hands. I begged for my brain to catch up and make something worthwhile come out of my mouth. I became a sputtering mess instead, telling her how much she influenced my life. I handed her a copy of my play, which I just "happened" to have in my purse because I knew that when I met her I wanted to give it to her. She graciously accepted it. I heard myself rambling on and on, telling her my entire life story. I wanted someone to say, "Shit! Trey, put a damn sock in it already!" But I had a severe case of diarrhea of the mouth. Oprah nodded and tried her best to hear me out, but I could see she was eying the exit. And I didn't blame her! Oprah graciously cut me off, wished me well with my career, and excused herself. In shock I watched her exit, knowing I had just blown it! I looked like a deranged lunatic. How could I blow a meeting with Oprah? But I did! My biggest takeaway from that was to be specific when asking for something from the Universe. I wanted to meet Oprah. And the Universe made that happen, but I needed to be clear. What I should have requested was (and I now always state my wishes as if they already manifested), "Dear Universe, I'm thrilled to have a calm, wonderful, inspiring conversation with Oprah. She is inspired by my story and wants to hear more!" If there is ever a moment in my entire life that I wish I could do over, that is it. But it was also a valuable lesson for me to show that when you put things into the Universe, the Universe will make it happen. Just be *fully* prepared for the results!

I believe in the power of the Universe. I believe in boldly asking it for what you want! Girl, I'm telling you, you need to have daily discussions with God/Universe. You also need to write shit down! Write down your dreams and goals. You need to have a positive mindset and believe anything is possible! But don't just write it down and think about it. You have to take planned actionable steps toward your goals while holding on to the faith that your goals are going to eventually happen. They may not happen on the timeline that you planned, but when they do, it will blow your mind! There is another affirmation that I regularly say when I want God to give me some direction on what needs to happen and I'm not sure if what I'm asking for is indeed the right thing for me. I often will say to the Universe, "God, if not this, and not now, then I will remain faithful and blessed because I know you have something better planned for me." That way, I'm able to let go of disappointment when it shows up in my life, and I don't spend my time obsessing over why something happened or why something didn't go according to plan. I know that eventually, it will all make sense.

Along with visualizing and manifesting, you must be careful of how you talk to yourself and realize that the voice you hear inside your head may not be yours. As much as my grandmother uplifted me with grandiose talk of how lucky I was, on the flip side of that, she also instilled in me lots of insecurities about my body and my features. My grandmother was a light-skinned Black woman, and so was my mother. Often, my grandmother would shake her head, look at me with clear disdain, and state, "I don't know why your mother decided to mix herself up with Black people. Anything too Black isn't good." The extra 20 or 30 pounds I carried around only added to her disdain. She would often say, "Well, if you're not pretty, at least you're smart!"

She promised that once I turned 16, she would save up enough money to get me a nose job. Often, she would walk up to me and pinch the bridge of my nose and nostrils and tell me to do that daily so it would help make my nose smaller and straighter. Yet no matter how many times per day I did it, it didn't make much of a difference. So I held on to the hope that things would be better once I turned 16. When I did turn 16, I was quite disappointed that my grandmother did not make good on her promise. I walked around thinking my big nose was out of place on my face and my darker skin wasn't something to be valued. I clearly saw how the girls and women in my family who had lighter skin were treated. If a baby was born into the family, the discussion usually focused on "how white" the baby looked or how "good" the baby's hair was. So, I got the message that I wasn't pretty, and I just accepted this as my lot in life.

I struggled with my weight, and my grandmother and mother were equally obsessed with not only my weight but also theirs. They ensured that as a family, we were always on a diet. So I did the cabbage soup diet, eating-only-pineapple diet, WeightWatchers, and Jenny Craig. We bonded over our dedication and willpower to stick to a diet and were fierce competitors in the weight-loss game. Whenever my grandmother called, she would ask, "Trey, so how is the weight?" as if it were an actual breathing person who lived in my house that she needed to inquire about! So it was no wonder that my dissatisfaction with my looks and body got worse before it got better. The constant dieting also led to me destroying my metabolism. By the time I was 30, I was 287 pounds! I opted for weight-loss surgery. It was a success, and I dropped the weight. At my lowest, I was a sleek size 4, but no matter how much weight I lost, I still loathed my body and myself. The negative self-talk was constant. I would stand in the mirror and nitpick everything. My stomach was still too big, my arms were too flabby, my nose too big for my face . . . The list was endless. And it didn't help that I was now on TV and all my co-stars were size 0–2. I was considered the "fat one" on the show, and I hated that my body didn't seem to want to conform to the ideals that I wanted. I wrote often about my body, describing my love/hate relationship with my boobs and other body parts. Here's one piece I wrote about my body for *Huffington Post*:

"The truth is I don't like my body. Not a big fan of her at all. I wouldn't willingly sign up for 'this,' or order this body. I would demand a refund! As a self-proclaimed feminist I struggle with this. Miss 'feminist,' burn your bra, loving all women and all of our sizes. Miss Trey Anthony, writer of 'Da Kink, the play that preaches self-acceptance and has women singing 'I'm just loving me!' doesn't like her body?

"And I've tried to practice what I preach to other women, about being okay with yourself. Loving yourself at whatever size you are, embracing all of you. And I honestly believe all of that, I really do. I just wish I could believe it for myself! My non-belief has made me do some mean and unhealthy things to myself to·achieve the 'perfect' body. I don't think there's a diet that I haven't tried. . . "

My constant dissatisfaction with my body would consume me. Every time I went to an event and someone took a picture, I worried about how fat I would look, and instead of enjoying the event, I would try to avoid the camera because I didn't want any unfavorable pictures of me showing up online. I would wear long sleeves during the summer, and I would be that girl at the party who refused to take her jacket off, while my slim friends dressed in short tank tops and cutoff jeans would be complaining about feeling too hot! Meanwhile I would be sweating buckets on the dance floor because I thought my arms were too fat. Black was my go-to color for everything. I always looked like I was on my way to a funeral. I would talk to my body like someone who could not stand the sight of me. It was awful. I avoided mirrors because God knows nothing had changed, and I hated watching myself on television. I would like to say that I had this breakthrough moment with my body, and one day I just stopped tearing it apart, but there wasn't. Rather, there was a quiet acceptance that this was indeed my body.

As I started to do inner healing work, I began to look at the way I spoke to myself and how critical I was. I began to do affirmations such as "I love and accept myself" or "Trey, you are worthy of love and compassion." As I continued to affirm myself, I began to feel more thankful for what my body could do versus what it couldn't do. I shifted my mindset from making my body smaller to wanting it to be stronger and healthier. I also began to appreciate my beauty when people told me I had a beautiful smile or big, beautiful eyes and gorgeous clear skin. Instead of ignoring them, I soaked in the praise. I began to see myself as pretty. Not beautiful but pretty. Someone who, on a good day, looked pretty damn good! I stopped the negative self-talk, I got my grandmother's voice out of my head, and I started to speak to myself as I would have wanted to speak to that nine-year-old Black girl who was waiting for someone to tell her she was beautiful. It's a journey. And, ladies, I will tell you, hitting the forties club makes you reevaluate your entire damn life. You start to not give a damn about reaching someone else's unrealistic expectations of who you are and what you are supposed to look like. Friends had warned me that once you hit 40, you start having less fucks to give, and they were right! And of course, there are days that I look in the mirror and think about packing this imperfect body up in a UPS box and returning it to the sender because this couldn't have been what I ordered! But most days, I'm better and I'm more intentional about shutting down the negative self-talk. I realize being a Black girl in love (with myself) means speaking kindly and softer to myself. It means being less judgmental and more forgiving.

So, sis, start to think about how you talk to yourself. What do you think about your body when you look in the mirror? What do you say to yourself? Would you say the same things to your best friend? If not, then stop speaking negatively to yourself. Take a closer look at yourself and focus on the things that you love. You do not have to fit the conventional constructs of Hollywood. As Lupita Nyong'o expressed in her interview for *Glamour* magazine, "There is room for diverse representation of beauty." Redefine it. Claim it. Own it. Tell other sisters when you see them how fierce they are with their Black girl magic, big afros, beautiful full lips, and glowing chocolate skin! Appreciate all of you and speak to yourself nicely! That's an order!

BLACK GIRL DREAMING: VISION BOARD:

The concept of the law of attraction might be met with some resistance. And, sis, I understand your skepticism about cutting out pictures, putting it on some construction paper, and then all of a sudden, your life is supposed to change! Girl, I can feel your eyes rolling. But what I do know is that for myself and the women I have worked with, having some version of a vision board has drastically improved their lives and given them something to use to hold themselves accountable. Every New Year's Eve, it has become a ritual for me to sit with some old *Essence* and *O* magazines, a pair of scissors, and a glue stick, and create a storybook of what I want to happen in my life. I try to focus on career, love, health, and family. I usually put this vision board somewhere I can see it. A good place for me is in my room, or I take a picture of it, and it's the screensaver on my phone. It is a constant reminder to me that these are the things that I want to manifest in my life. There is power in visualization, seeing something every day. Studies have shown that Olympic athletes who use visualization and visioning have been more successful. And it doesn't have to be this huge cardboard cutout above your bed. Sometimes, it can be something as simple as writing your vision on a Post-it Note and looking at it every day.

One of my favorite stories of the power of visualization is the story of comedian Jim Carrey. When he was a struggling comedian, he wrote himself a check for $10 million and signed it for service rendered. He carried it around in his wallet for years. When his big break came for the movie *Dumb and Dumber*, his fee, girl, was $10 million! Coincidence? I think not! When writing this chapter, I asked many folks to weigh in on vision boards. One of my good friends, Terri, shared that at the top of the year, she does one individually and one with her husband, and they revisit it throughout the year, helping them stay on track. Another friend, Leslie, shared that she writes down the most important things that she wants for the year, and she puts it in her Bible and prays over it daily. She sees that 90 percent of what she has written down usually comes true! Many shared that they like to look back on their vision board and see that what they put on it has actually become a reality. And who can forget Tererai Trent, who has been referred to as Oprah's favorite guest? While growing up poor in Zimbabwe, where girls were not allowed to get an education, her mother encouraged her to write down her dreams. She wrote down that she wanted to "one day work for the causes of women and girls in poverty." She placed the paper in a tin and buried it in the same place where she worked herding cattle. And she often thought about what she wrote, determined to make her dreams a reality. And they did come true: she is now a doctor, scholar, and humanitarian. A true source of inspiration to her entire village and country.

There is power in the pen. There is power in creating some sort of vision board. Write down what you want. Look at it daily. Think about it often. Take intentional steps to make it happen. Sis, you got this!

GETTING RID OF CLUTTER TO FIND OUT WHAT'S IMPORTANT

The Universe loves symbolic gestures. If you want more goodness in your life, you have to make room for it. Practice doing a clearing of your mind and your physical space. Just the act of getting rid of clutter and junk can have a tremendous impact on your well-being. Whenever

I start to feel overwhelmed, unclear, and imbalanced, I start to take a look at my physical surroundings. I start with my closet. What have I been saving or trying to eventually fit into? What is no longer my style? How many items in my closet have been on the same hangers for over a year and I still haven't worn them? I start to get rid of those things. When I started trying to save money so I could afford a full-time nanny, I began to see how little clothing I actually needed. Like most women, I tended to wear my go-to pieces and had a few signature items that were crowd favorites. Once I put a hold on spending on clothing, I didn't miss it.

When clients reach out to me and say they are feeling overwhelmed, I often give the simple assignment of first cleaning out their car, then their closet, and then another room in their house where they spend the most time. Usually, the act of physically clearing helps them deal with the mental clutter in their mind. I often get some of my best ideas while cleaning and often my clients tell me that a decluttered home makes them more relaxed and gives them a sense of clarity. I truly believe a cluttered home is representative of a cluttered mind.

When clearing my space, I often state the following affirmation: "I'm making room for new, wonderful, and delicious things to enter my life!" And if you're a paper pack rat like me, please spend some time going through all your old papers and items and *stop* taking new ones. When people try to hand me flyers and business cards, I say no. I often tell them to text me the info or send me an e-flyer. That way I don't bring unnecessary clutter into my life.

Sis, for the next 30 days, don't buy anything new, unless it's groceries. Also, don't bring any extra paper into your home, including magazines and flyers. And pick one room, drawer, or closet to declutter. See how you feel once you start clearing away the blocks to your blessings.

SIS, GET YOUR MIND RIGHT!

1. Write down in your journal critical things you were told about yourself as a child and how those beliefs affect you now as an adult.

2. Write down three affirmations you can use for active mirror work to help combat negative self-talk.

3. Get an accountability partner and set a date for you to start a vision board. It doesn't matter what time of the year it is. Then, create your vision board. If you have one already, revisit it and see what things can be updated and what intentional steps you can take to make some things on your vision board come true.

affirmations

I LOVE MY BODY AND I TREAT IT WITH CARE.

THE UNIVERSE IS ALWAYS WORKING ON ADDITIONAL WAYS TO MAKE MY DREAMS COME TRUE.

LIFE LOVES ME AND FULLY SUPPORTS ME.

chapter 11

Love, Sex, and Intimacy

BLACK GIRL PLAYLIST:
"LET'S TALK ABOUT SEX,"
SALT-N-PEPA

I was 10 years old when I got my period. I knew what it was because our fifth-grade health teacher had been very thorough about giving us an example using ketchup poured on thick maxi pads to ensure we knew what to expect. So I was on the lookout but not as prepared as I thought. Unlucky for me, my very first period came in swimming class, in the pool, and I thought Jaws had struck. I was convinced my days were over, and I screamed hysterically, searching for the big white shark that had entered the pool! My quick-thinking gym teacher ran to my aid and told me to exit the pool as the rest of my class stood around and giggled. In the changing room, she gave me a single box of Dr. White's pads, told me to stick it inside my underwear, and that was that.

I felt a sense of relief and pride. A pride that among my peer group, I was the first one to get my period. I ran home and shared the news with my grandmother, who was cooking dinner in the kitchen. My grandmother slammed the pot lid down and looked me up and down. Her eyes burned with anger. "So you tink you're a woman now! How dare you come in here with a period at your age! You better learn to keep your legs closed because I won't be looking after no baby!" My poor little brain couldn't comprehend why she was so angry and how having a period could lead you to having a baby. I was too scared to ask my grandmother to explain this because I knew somehow I was to blame for this period happening. Later that night, my grandmother silently placed a box of pads on my bed. I knew better than to say a word. And that was all the discussion we ever had about sex, periods, and babies.

And I felt that my body continued to betray me. By the time I was 11, I was fully developed and unprepared to deal with the looks and advances that came from boys and grown-ass men who should have known better. Boys constantly pulled on my bra strap and tried to grope me. I was embarrassed by my full breasts, and I tried to wear baggy clothing to hide them. My grandmother monitored my developing body with a mixture of disdain and concern, which added to my shame and my belief that I was the one responsible for the lustful response that men and boys now had toward me. But my grandmother couldn't protect me from an older neighbor, "Uncle Henry," who, while my grandmother was in bed having one of her depressive episodes, used that opportunity to grope my breasts and stick his tongue in my mouth. I stood there, frozen, as I floated above my body as his tongue searched for mine. I was in shock and had enough sense to tell my grandmother and uncles. Luckily, I was believed, and my uncles went to Uncle Henry's house. Rumor has it that they beat him up or ran him out of town or more. I really don't know what happened, but I do know that I never saw him again. But my grandmother was not satisfied. She laid down the law. I was now forbidden to leave the house unless accompanied by a family member—and no more playing outside unattended. I thought that I was to blame for men's lustful response to my body.

At 12 years old, I was sent to Canada to live with my mother. My youthful mother had a more liberal approach to sexuality and tried to be my "cool best friend." She attempted to engage me in conversation about sex, but by then, I was too ashamed, and I shut down all her attempts, figuring that it was a little too late now. By 15, I had my first serious boyfriend. Both of us were virgins, and his best friend was also dating my best friend. The four of us decided it was time for us to lose our virginity, so we selected a firm date. We also knew the deed could happen at my house because my mother was busy working her three jobs, and I knew for sure she wouldn't be home. The day I lost my virginity, I remember lying there and thinking I wasn't sure what all the hype was about. Sex was okay but not a big deal. I exchanged notes with my best friend. She was underwhelmed as well, and we were both confused. My boyfriend seemed to enjoy it more than I did, and so for the next three years of our relationship, we continued. I never questioned if I was supposed to be getting pleasure, and he never asked. I genuinely thought sex was an expectation that needed to be met to make your boyfriend happy, and no one told me any different.

It wasn't until my late twenties that I found an amazing, loving partner who was committed to my enjoyment during sex. He asked questions that we explored together, and during the seven years we were in a relationship, he made sex and intimacy an equal partnership. It was in this relationship that I became fully empowered: I wasn't scared to ask for what I wanted, and I enjoyed learning various ways to please my partner and myself. And for once in my life, I felt as if I had full ownership of my body and emotions, and it was okay for me to feel desire and lust, and to be able to act on my feelings without any shame. I became a liberated, sexual being and an outspoken advocate for women to embrace their sensuality.

AUNT JEMIMA ISN'T WEARING A THONG!

Black women are fighting several stereotypes pertaining to our sexuality and sensuality. We have the oversexed Black woman who is popping out children every hour! Or she appears oversexed again in a music video where she has one too many bottles of champagne poured over her breasts while another rapper taps her big, voluptuous ass. And then, of course, there's the asexual Aunt Jemima type who for sure ain't getting any and is just happy being in the kitchen singing church hymns. So no wonder many of us have a complicated relationship with sex and our bodies.

Yet, to be a Black woman (in love with yourself), you must closely examine your relationship to sex, intimacy, and romantic partnership. Did you grow up in a household where sex wasn't discussed? Were your sexual boundaries exploited by adults, so you now still need to work through that trauma and the guilt that accompanies it? How does religion play into your sexual beliefs and comfort? Were you raised that "good" girls don't have sex until marriage? And did you believe that, or did you rebel, having many sexual partners because you wanted to get back at your parents? I always encourage women to take some time to reflect on their attitudes about sex. Exploring your relationship to sex through therapy can also help.

GIRL, TOUCH IT! YES, SIS, YOU CAN!

If you are a single lady, there is no better time to be having sex—great sex—by yourself. Take this time to explore your body. Find out what ways can make you reach the big O! How do you like to be touched? What things turn you on? Do you like visual intimacy, physical intimacy, dirty talk, toys, fingers? Maybe a bit of everything? Do you enjoy reading erotica, watching porn, and getting sensual massages? Explore. Love on your body. Get comfortable with touching yourself intimately. A lot of times, when we are single, we believe that intimacy can only occur in a partnership or with another person, but it's important to figure out what you like so you can confidently share that information with someone else.

BUY YOUR OWN DAMN FLOWERS!

When I was in a relationship, my partner would often surprise me with flowers. I loved coming home to roses in the kitchen or in the bedroom. Once that relationship ended, so did the flower buying. It didn't occur to me that I could also buy myself flowers until one day, a friend came over and bought me a pretty orchid, and I remembered how much I loved fresh flowers in the house. My friend shared that she often bought flowers for herself. Her sharing this information gave me the obvious permission to start doing the same. It was a way to show love and appreciation to myself. I also started buying candles and lighting them. Taking long, luxurious baths with scented candles became my favorite thing. And after my bath, I would use my favorite scented lotions to give myself a slow sensuous massage and spend a little intimate time with myself.

I realized that intimacy and love didn't have to always involve another person and that I could fall in love with myself and treat myself the way I wanted a partner to. I was learning how to physically and emotionally take care of myself. I was also preparing myself and my body for when my ideal partner shows up.

We need to get rid of the notion that romance, love, and intimacy can only be created when you are in a partnership. Often, when clients come to see me and they complain about wanting a partner, I encourage them to start the romance with themselves; it gives the Universe a clear example of what you are indeed looking for.

I share with them that I often do mirror work by looking into my own eyes and stating, "I love you, Trey." The first time I did this, I broke down crying, and it took several attempts for me to be able to make eye contact with myself. The most empowering thing a woman can do for herself is to understand that intimacy and love are things that she can give herself.

If you are in a relationship, be intentional about creating an intimacy that doesn't always involve sexual intercourse. You and your partner could give each other facials. There is such intimacy in massaging or touching someone's face. Another way to create intimacy is to sit cross-legged on the floor, facing each other, and stare into each other's eyes. Do this three times in three-minute intervals. Don't be surprised if you become emotional while looking at each other. After you finish this exercise with your partner, talk about your childhood and your childhood ideals of what love meant to you. Ask your partner about their first kiss, their first orgasm, the first time they masturbated. These exercises require a deep sense of trust and vulnerability because you may be sharing information that you haven't told anyone else. And often talking about masturbation can make you feel uncomfortable, but trust the process and realize that discussing how you give yourself pleasure is nothing to be ashamed of.

SEX AND AGING

I recently did a live show on Instagram about sex and Black women. I was interviewing two Black sex experts, and before the show, I asked viewers to submit questions. I was surprised by how many middle-aged women were unaware of the changes that can happen in our bodies as we age and how they can affect our sexual desires. We also do not understand how diet, exercise, and stress can impact our relationship with our bodies and how much energy we may or may not have to engage in sexual intimacy. Many of us are so used to being tired and still getting up to get shit done that we don't recognize when our tiredness has peaked to exhaustion. We are so busy putting others first that we do not go to a doctor to discuss our concerns. Also, if the person in the white coat doesn't look like us, we may find it hard to address or share some of our medical concerns. I recently moved and needed to find a gynecologist who was located closer to my home. When I was calling around, I just requested a female doctor. Thus, I was pleasantly surprised, upon arriving for my appointment, to find out that my new doctor was a Black woman. In the past, all my doctors had been white men. My appointment with my new doctor was like no other;

there was an ease and comfort that we immediately had. When we discussed the medical history of my family and some of my concerns, she nodded her head in knowing agreement, expressing a sistahood that showed she understood how being a Black woman also affected my physical and emotional well-being. I usually have a hard time with pap smears and have found them extremely uncomfortable and painful. However, my new doctor talked me through it, she was gentle and informative, and for once, I felt truly seen. When she said the pap smear was complete, I was in shock. I barely felt a thing. It was the best damn appointment in my life. Maybe she's just a damn good doctor who happens to be a Black woman, but for me, I didn't realize how important it was to have a doctor who looks like me and could actually relate to some of my experiences. I strongly encourage you to seek out Black female medical professionals if possible, to see if it makes a difference in your care.

SIS, GET YOUR MIND RIGHT!

1. Write down what intimacy and love look like currently in your life.

2. Write down how you would like that to change.

3. If you're in a partnership, set a date with your partner to have a night of intimacy that does not include sex. If you are single, set a date for yourself and prepare for an intimate night alone. What do you need? Candles? Bubble bath? Lotion?

affirmations

I'M WORTHY OF LOVE, TENDERNESS,
AND INTIMACY IN MY LIFE.

I LOVE AND ACCEPT MYSELF.

THE UNIVERSE IS BRINGING MY PERFECT MATE TO ME.

chapter 12

Black Women and Vulnerability

BLACK GIRL PLAYLIST:
"I AM LIGHT,"
INDIA ARIE

When I was nine years old and living in England, my mother left my brother and me with our grandmother and moved to Canada for a new job. My grandmother was now the primary caregiver of two additional children while still taking care of several of her own children who still resided in the home. Money was tight, but my grandmother always ensured that we had food in the house. She made a big deal of always cooking a big pot of rice and peas and chicken for Sunday dinner, complete with a freshly made apple pie or blackberry pie with fresh custard that we washed down with some carrot juice. To this day, I have a hard time eating alone because I find myself mourning the loss of my big family dinners.

Mealtime was very important to my grandmother, and my grandmother took great pride in always having her fridge overflowing with food and our bellies full. She would beam at the entire family as she saw us heap spoons of rice onto our already overflowing plates or argue about who was going to have the extra chicken leg. From her, I grew up knowing that food was equated with love and family.

However, one day before class, my teacher pulled me aside and expressed her concern about the growing stress being placed on my grandmother because of having "two extra mouths to feed." With a look of pity and concern, she handed me a form to take home to my grandmother that would qualify my brother and me for free lunches. The teacher stressed that my grandmother would no longer have to give my brother and me weekly lunch money. I eagerly ran home with the form, and I thought my grandmother would be as delighted as I was that she could save more money. However, she was far from happy. My grandmother took one look at the form and ripped it up. She was raging as she expressed, "Tell your little so-called teacher to not feel sorry for me! We do not need her handouts! We have more than enough! Dis family is not a charity case!"

My nine-year-old self could not understand why my grandmother was so upset, but what I now understand is that it was unacceptable to her to take money from anyone and that she believed you shouldn't let people feel sorry for you. People offering you help was not a good thing.

Fast forward 30 years, and I'm now in the biggest crisis of my life. I'm no longer in a high two-income household. I'm suddenly single, dealing with an earth-shattering breakup. I have a newborn baby, and my income seems to be rapidly decreasing by the minute because the world is now in a global pandemic. My shows, workshops, and talks are being canceled as the government informs us to stay home. I'm an emotional wreck, stressed, and feeling the walls caving in on me. Thankfully I have some savings, but I'm carefully monitoring my money, and I'm painfully aware that I'm spending and not making any additional income. This begins to stress me even more. Thank God I have the insight to take my own advice and begin seeing a therapist. But it isn't cheap. Each session costs me $150 per hour, and as much as I know that I emotionally need this, I cannot justify spending this amount on a weekly session as I watch income I thought I could count on magically disappear. The world is in shock, the economy is at a standstill, and there is no end in sight. No one seems to know when things will return to normal. As I start to scrutinize my budget, I know that my weekly therapy sessions have to go. I compromise with myself, saying that I will cut them down to one session every three weeks. I know it's a sacrifice that I have to make to stay afloat.

I'm on the phone with my dear friend Rel, who is doing her weekly check-in sessions with me. She knows I'm still mourning the loss of my relationship and I'm still feeling overwhelmed by motherhood. She gently inquires how I am doing. Despite my best efforts, I start crying. Rel calmly soothes me and asks how my new weekly therapy sessions are going. I tell her that they are going well, but due to my concerns about my income, I have cut them down. Without skipping a beat, Rel says, "You are going through an awful breakup. You have just moved. You are a new mother. We are in a pandemic. If a person were experiencing one of these things, it would be stressful;

you are experiencing all these things simultaneously. You are going through extreme trauma. Please send me your account number. Sheila [her partner] and I will pay for the extra sessions. You need them. We can't afford to lose you—you're too important to many people. And I know you would have done the same for me. I will send you the money."

All of a sudden, I'm nine years old, back in my grandmother's kitchen. I feel her rage. I'm seeing her rip up the free lunch paper. I don't want anyone feeling sorry for me—I'm not someone's charity case! I quickly refuse. Assuring Rel that I'm fine, I don't need help. Rel is firm. She begs me to take some time to think about it before saying no. I quickly get off the phone and then I sit with her offer. I feel shame. I cry. I think some more. This is more than generous. I'm blessed to have such amazing friends. I sit with my own shame, now alongside gratitude. What does this mean if I accept it? Taking money from her makes me feel vulnerable. Taking money for extra therapy confirms to that critical voice in my head that I'm weak. How dare I take money for something as "frivolous" as therapy. My poor granny must be rolling in her grave! I rock my newborn son in my arms as I think it over. I look down at his innocent face. He has a blind trust and knows and understands that I will take care of him. I know he deserves to have a mother who is emotionally prepared to be a mother. He deserves a mother who prioritizes her own well-being, and that means she can assess when she needs help. In my own childhood, I carried the burden of misplaced trauma and stress. When the Black women in my family were overburdened, emotionally drained, and feeling unsupported, they took their frustration out on me. I know what it feels like to be viewed as one more thing to do on their overflowing to-do list.

I smile down at my son. I'm not weak. I am not a charity case. I deserve support. I deserve help. I deserve love. I need to do this for my son and myself. I pick up my phone and text Rel my account details. I thank the Universe for sending me grace, compassion, and love.

Too many of us struggle with the facade we share with the public. And yet there are the realities of our lives. I had the pleasure of interviewing Dr. LaShawnDa Pittman during my research for this book. She has a Ph.D. in Sociology and has conducted extensive research pertaining to Black women and vulnerability. Dr. Pittman shared how vulnerability showed up for many Black women when it comes to finances and how many of us do not share our financial concerns due to shame. "As Black women, we are more likely than our white counterparts to experience financial struggle, to be raising our children alone. And although we work more than white women, we earn less than white women on average, not to mention all men. We are more likely to be family and community caregivers than other women. To be doing time with incarcerated loved ones. So, essentially we are doing more with less."

During our interview, I could not help but think about my poor grandmother doing more with less.

Every Sunday she got up early to cook dinner, and we would leave about 8 A.M. to visit my uncle, who was in prison. We would drive for nearly two hours, and my grandmother would refer to me as "her little company." She didn't have her driver's license—she had failed the driving test seven times, but that didn't stop her! So, for all my life, my gangster granny was driving dirty! I was her co-pilot, and I would tell her when it was safe for her to change lanes on the highway. We would sing along to the radio, and I would write songs and stories in my notebook and read them aloud to her, and my grandmother would add to the story plot. Often, my grandmother would inappropriately share all the family gossip and tell me to add that to the story. I enjoyed going on these long drives with her. It was truly our bonding time.

Eventually we would arrive at the prison, and my grandmother enjoyed chatting with the other women while we waited in a long line outside. Most of them bonded around the disappointment of having sons, husbands, or fathers behind bars. Once the gate was opened, we would sign in and security would pat us down. We would then sit in a big waiting room. Sometimes, my uncle came out quickly; other times, we sat there for hours until a prison officer led him and he swaggered toward us. I used to think he looked so cool in his baggy blue overalls and white tennis shoes, and he always seemed happy to see us. My grandmother would not make eye contact with her son. No hugging was allowed, but even if it was, we knew my grandmother wasn't the hugging type. She was stoic and kissed her teeth as he sat down. She would shoot him a quick, disapproving look before reaching into her big black handbag and handing my uncle a big plastic ice cream container that now served as Tupperware, filled with rice and peas and stewed chicken and my grandmother's famous coleslaw. My grateful uncle would gobble it down as my grandmother intensely watched. I would fill in the awkward silence by giving my uncle amusing play-by-play about what was happening at home or sharing all the family drama that my grandmother had recently told me. I honestly feel this is how I learned to keep an audience captive!

Thirty minutes later, the visit would abruptly end. A guard would tap my uncle on the shoulder and lead him away. My grandmother, with her head held high, would pop the empty container back in her handbag and silently motion for me to follow her. We would head home, driving for another two hours. During the ride home, she would barely say a word. And I would instinctively know that my role was to be silent and only tell her when to change lanes. Once we arrived home, my grandmother would warm up the pots on the stove. She would have Sunday dinner with the rest of the family, wash the dishes, and then she would sleep for a short while and head to her night shift.

Now, as a grown woman, I reflect on the emotional toll of this Sunday morning journey for my grandmother. How it must have felt for her to see her youngest son behind bars and not be allowed to touch him. I think of her sacrifice. How she expressed her love by bringing him food. How she never cried, never showed any emotions. How she never brought along another adult or family member for comfort. How she could only trust and rely on her nine-year-old granddaughter for company. How she risked driving every Sunday with no driver's license to see her son. How, as Black women, we will find a way even when there seems to be none. It makes me weep. Even writing this makes me weep. I ache for her. I wish I could have done more for her than tell her that it was safe to change lanes. I often wonder about the times when my grandmother headed to bed and pulled the covers up around her head. Was this the time she faced her own notion of vulnerability? Did she cry underneath those covers, not trusting that anyone would be capable of sharing her pain and burden?

Many of us are navigating less-than-ideal circumstances and harsh realities. Yet we still want to be viewed as strong, capable women. We do not know how to be vulnerable. We do not know how to deal with the emotions that come up for us if we are vulnerable. We can watch all the Brené Brown videos on vulnerability, but we also have deep-rooted trust issues. Some of us have attempted to trust partners, friends, and loved ones and have found ourselves holding the huge pile of poop, otherwise known as the letdown bag, when we had our vulnerability thrown in our face. When I was dumped by my ex, I couldn't help but feel duped for fully trusting someone and believing they would hold my trust sacred. I was mad at myself for walking into this relationship arms and heart wide open and believing her when she swore up and down that she would always be there for me. I battled with myself for a long time about how much I would reveal in future relationships, and I was tempted to start rebuilding the walls around my heart because I never wanted to feel hurt like that again. I knew I could never survive another betrayal like that.

During this time, my mother was quick to once again offer her unsolicited advice. "Trey, your problem is you give too much. You give too much of yourself over to others." In other words, my mother thought I was too vulnerable and that vulnerability could only lead to tremendous hurt. And as tempting as it was to restart the narrative in my head that people couldn't be trusted, that loving someone could only lead to hurt, or that accepting money from people could only lead to them later having something to throw in my face, I decided that my ex was only one person. Yes, she had let me down, and perhaps I had misplaced my trust. I had given too much to the wrong person. I expressed my fears about love to a close friend who simply stated, "Don't let this experience change you; people love you because you show up fully to love. You picked wrong this time but trust that next time you will pick right."

I knew there were people in my life whom I could trust. I also knew that to find the love I wanted, I needed to show up healed, open, compassionate, and kind. Because we attract what we are. So instead of shutting down my vulnerability, I worked on becoming more vulnerable. Instead of telling people I was fine, I shared my hurt, frustration, and disappointment. I decided to write and share my biggest vulnerabilities in this book to also help other Black women know that it is okay to take off your superwoman cape.

A few weeks before this book was due to the editor, I suffered another loss. A friend suddenly died. She was young, only 42, and a mother of two. She was a go-getter, a woman who I would often turn to for a pep talk. I was devastated by her loss. And instead of dealing with the various emotions that her death brought up for me, I chose to do what many of us do: I buried myself in my work. I also decided that an entire pan of homemade brownies and a tub of toasted caramel ice cream should do the trick! I swallowed every emotion that I should be feeling. I told myself I didn't have the time or energy to grieve. I went into survival mode. I had work deadlines to meet. A damn book to turn in on how we Black women needed to take better care of ourselves and make time for ourselves. The irony wasn't lost on me and while sitting at my computer, I just broke down. I slammed my computer shut and spoke to that little girl in me who was feeling scared, who missed her friend, who wished that she had called her more often, who was now worried about her own mortality, who was worried that she would not be around to see her child grow up. I gave myself permission to grieve and took three days off. During that time, I ensured that I took daily walks and I meditated. I cried. I reached out to friends. I publicly acknowledged my feelings on social media and told people I was devastated and needed to sit with my emotions. The post was flooded with comments from other community members who also expressed their grief. A group of my friend's super-duper high-achieving Black women formed a group on Facebook where we helped each other through our grief. We showed up in our most vulnerable state and became true supporters for one another. I realized that by allowing myself to be vulnerable, it gave others permission to do so as well.

I understand vulnerability is hard for us because many of us have been raised by women who never cried, never showed they were scared, never asked for help or support. So we need to be intentional with our efforts to work on this and actively changing this herstory in our families. There is no need to compare our lives with our mothers and grandmothers. Maybe, in some respects, our mothers and grandmothers had it harder, but does that mean we are not allowed to express hurt, pain, or fear? We have to sit with the questions, What does true vulnerability look like for me? Who can I trust to show up for me? Starting today, who will I let in? Also, think about how you can encourage other Black women in your life to be more vulnerable. Usually, vulnerability has a ripple effect—the more you share, the more others will feel comfortable to truly be themselves as well.

RAISING VULNERABLE CHILDREN

The running joke within our family is that my mother can be dead wrong about something, and even if Jesus Christ jumped off the cross and told her she was wrong, she would never admit it. My mother can cuss you out, give you the silent treatment, find out she was wrong about what she cussed you out for, and then will just show up at your house, put on the kettle, make herself a cup of tea, and act like nothing happened. My dad is somewhat less temperamental and a quiet fellow. However, there are no apologies, and no I love yous. I speak to my dad on the phone about twice per month, and he would end every conversation with "Okay, be good." I know this is his version of "I love you." I know both of my parents grew up with parents who didn't tell them, "I love you." This was deemed too vulnerable, not necessary, or something that only white folks do.

However, six years ago, when my nephew was born, it shifted the dynamics within our family. My sister and her husband—dedicated, millennial, first-time parents— rolled in a new game plan. We watched with bated breath and disbelief when they shared with our jaded family how they now believed in discussing feelings, giving their son options, and time outs versus a whooping. My mother raised her eyebrow. She knew the devil was hard at work, and she wasn't wrong, as this child burst out on our family scene with an expectation to hear "I love you," "I'm sorry," and "I was wrong." And surprise, he was the first one to check my mother and tell her, "Hey, Grandma, that hurt my feelings. You need to say I'm sorry." And without hesitation, our stubborn, West Indian mother would quickly apologize to her only grandchild and take his feelings into consideration. Who the hell was this woman? And where had she been all my damn life? Now she was even throwing in "I love you" after every call with her precious grandson. This left us all scratching our heads and getting all up in our feelings. The surprising paradigm shift with my mother made me realize that vulnerability can be taught at any age, and children can be our biggest teacher if we allow them.

Yet I know as a community, we often associate vulnerability with weakness. I once attended a comedy show, and a famous comedian did a bit about waking his son up every day and just punching him in the face. He said he needed to prepare him for the realities of being a Black man where shit will just happen to you for no reason. And besides, he didn't want his kid to grow up "soft" and wanting to talk about feelings. The audience was killing themselves with laughter. And I couldn't help but recall several occasions as a child, being on the brink of crying and holding in my tears as I was threatened by my mother and grandmother with the classic cautionary Black saying, "Do you want me to give you something to cry for?" I would immediately bite my lip and swallow down every emotion. Again, I was being taught that there was no room for emotions; no one would allow space for me to be vulnerable. When my sister went on her honeymoon, my mother and I took turns looking after my nephew. One night he became quite emotional, talking about missing his parents. I held space for him. I told him it was okay to feel sad about missing his parents. I held him and cuddled with him in bed, and he looked up at me and said, "Auntie Trey, you are really good at listening to my feelings. You made me feel better." I got choked up knowing that even now, as a grown woman, this is what I would have wanted. Just imagine if when we were children, we were given the space and opportunities to safely express our emotions and vulnerability. By the time we reached adulthood, we would then have developed the self-awareness to be able to express our emotions instead of viewing vulnerability as weakness or unnecessary. And maybe more of us would be less defensive, less suspicious, and less distrustful of others, and more in tune with our emotions.

We need to be deliberate and intentional with our vulnerability. When friends call or text me and ask, "How are you?" I no longer go to the tried and true answer of "I'm fine." I actually give them a balanced representation of my life. Often, I will respond with something like, "Doing good! Just booked another talk and got a great review of my play. But yesterday I ate my emotions again and had a bowl of brownies and ice cream for dinner. I recognize I overate because I felt like a lousy mom because I put the kid to bed without giving him a bath or reading him a book. I woke up with extreme mommy guilt. Do you ever feel guilty about not getting this motherhood shit right?"

By being vulnerable, honest, and open, I allow the people in my life to engage with the true me. If I had just stopped at "I'm doing good! Just booked another talk and got a great review of my play"—something I would have done in the past—it would set up the illusion of me having the perfect life or being a superwoman, holding it all together. I no longer wish to present like that. I want to celebrate my successes, but I also want my loved ones to know that I struggle with various things and I'm seeking support and validation for my struggles.

SIS, GET YOUR MIND RIGHT!

1. In your journal write down an instance when you were vulnerable and it backfired.

2. Write down the ways you can be more vulnerable with yourself, friends, and other meaningful relationships in your life.

3. Write a short poem or note to the scared little girl inside you, comforting her the way you would want someone to comfort you.

affirmations

LIFE PROTECTS AND SUPPORTS ME AT ALL TIMES.

I TRUST THAT OTHERS WILL ALWAYS BE AVAILABLE TO LOVE AND SUPPORT ME.

I SHOW UP AS MY AUTHENTIC SELF AT ALL TIMES.

chapter 13

Keep 'da Faith, Girl

Black Girl Playlist:
"Jesus Walks,"
Kanye West

My auntie Pat is a devout Christian—a Bible always close by, head covered, long skirts, very pious. She is our family's moral compass, and she is known to send a Bible scripture in the family's WhatsApp group to keep all our asses in check. However, rumor has it that in her heyday, she won the coveted title of Miss Hot Pants, but I can't picture it. To me, she is the person who taught me the most about faith, God, and religion. My grandmother and mother weren't that religious. My mother attended church maybe on Christmas and Easter, and my grandmother had a true disdain for the church, always thinking that the pastor was ripping off the congregation. So as a little girl, whenever we went up to Auntie Pat's, I looked forward to jumping on the church bus in my fancy dress and a small beret and going to the all-day conventions. I also loved flirting with all the cute boys, but that's another story for another time. But I genuinely loved the frenzy of the church—the booming choir, women swaying wildly to the music as they shook their tambourines, and people catching the spirits, falling to the ground as the pastor feverishly preached from the pulpit and begged people to come to the altar to save their lost souls. I would get caught up in it all, and in the church, I definitely felt a direct connection to God, and somehow, I believed that if I prayed in the church, everything I prayed for would be answered. While in church, I would drop to my knees and have long conversations with God, and I would feel a calmness overtake me, and I knew that God was hearing me. I loved the church and was quite annoyed that my mother and grandmother wouldn't let me go more often. However, as much as I begged to go to church when I was younger, as an adult, I've taken on the church-going habits of my mother and grandmother and only attend occasionally—but what remained was my faith in prayer.

In the past when I struggled with my sexuality and queer identity, I also struggled with my faith. How could I have a relationship with God/Universe when people found it necessary to recite biblical verses to condemn me. For this reason I stayed away from many traditional churches. I knew that religion didn't fully feel right for me. However each morning I try to listen to faith leaders that seem more inclusive such as Sarah Jakes Roberts, T.D. Jakes, and Toure Roberts. And some mornings I listen to Les Brown and Tony Robbins. I also have embraced more New Thought leaders such as Louise Hay, Wayne Dyer, and Deepak Chopra; their work spoke to me on a deeper level that seemed to sit right with my soul. The book *You Can Heal Your Life* by Louise Hay became my moral compass. The teachers who practiced New Thought thinking seemed more inclusive, and I knew that I had found my spiritual home within this methodology. I also was very interested in Buddhism, and I began reading a lot of books about it. I felt a connection with the Buddhist beliefs that nothing is fixed or permanent. Many of the practices spoke to me. So I took what worked from Buddhism and New Thought thinking and Christianity and came up with my own practice that works for me. I now pray, I meditate, I light candles, I burn incense, and I sometimes read Bible scriptures alongside reading *You Can Heal Your Life*. I read affirmation cards. I try my best to leave people better than I found them. I work on being soft and gentle with myself and others. I focus on forgiveness rather than revenge, and I know that God walks with me daily. During every dark moment in my life, from walking away from a seven-year relationship, to the death of my grandmother, to the demise of a primary business relationship, I have leaned heavily on my faith. I have dropped to my knees and each time, God has reassured me that "he's got this" and I need to share my path, my lesson with the world. Again, my mess would be my message. I have this inner peace, this inner quiet, this knowing that all is well, and this too shall pass. I know that God will never forsake me, and it's up to me to hold on to faith and see the glimpses of light that the Universe offers me in the darkness. That light will lead me to where I need to be.

As Black women, many of us are raised by praying grandmothers who have encouraged us to take our troubles to the Lord. Our religion, spirituality, faith, and prayers have seen us through many crises. And I do take my troubles to God. I pray daily. One of my most favorite prayers I recite often, and I believe I heard Oprah say it, or maybe it was a I-loved-it-and-I-sort-of-made-up-my-own-version prayer: "God, please grant me the clarity and insight to do your work. Please tell me, Where is it you want me to go? What it is you want me to say and to whom? Because I can do all things through you." I believe that God/Universe has an assignment for all of our lives. There is a purpose with your name on it. And it's our job to ask God for guidance to pursue the mission that God has laid out for us. I'm also a believer that everything happens for a reason, and as painful as some moments have been in my life, I hold on to that reasoning. That there must be a lesson to be learned in every situation that has caused hurt, pain, turmoil, or confusion. At these times, it is a moment to dig deeper, to go within and find out how or why you attracted this situation to your life. Also, my love for gospel music has helped me get through some moments. There's nothing like a good ole Kirk Franklin "Stomp" to let me know that God's got me. When I was going through my awful breakup, every morning in the shower, I would play that song. The lyrics reminded me that even though I was going through some hard things, God would change the direction of my life. I directly called on the Universe to help me make sense of everything that was going on. And even in my darkest hour, I knew that I was going to look back at this period of transition in my life and be thankful for it, and I had faith that I would make it to the other side, better and wiser for it.

Prayer is an important part of my life as well as daily affirmations. I receive daily affirmation texts on my phone, and I love to draw a card from my Louise Hay affirmation card deck. I regularly use angel cards as well, and before drawing one, I ask the angels what message they would like for me to know. I use the card that I draw as daily inspiration and guidance for the day.

I have had many people remark on my eternal optimism and positive attitude, and those things are directly linked to my belief that God/Universe is going to make a way for me. And of course, I have my moments of doubt, but I'm intentional about not dwelling in negativity. And when I get despondent, I often think about past experiences where I was convinced that this was the horrible experience that would threaten to take me out. Yet, somehow, I always made it through. Somehow, I always got back up. Somehow, I walked through the darkness and found the light.

SIS, GET YOUR MIND RIGHT!

1. How has spirituality shown up in your life?

2. Do you find your spiritual life fulfilling? If not, how can you change that?

3. When do you feel the closest to the Universe/God? In church? In nature? In the quiet moments before the world fully wakes up?

4. Write down a dark moment that you thought you would never get through. What did you learn from that moment? Did your faith get you through? How so?

affirmations

THE UNIVERSE HAS MY BACK AT ALL TIMES.

THIS TOO SHALL PASS.

GOD OPENS ALL DOORS THAT ARE MEANT TO BE MY DOORS!

chapter 14

Daddy Issues!

Black Girl Playlist: "Dance with My Father," Luther Vandross

I had gotten to nearly the end of the book, and I was unsure about whether to write a chapter about Black women and our fathers. I debated back and forth about how Black fathers factor into our journey to self-love. To be quite honest, I wasn't sure if I had the insight, knowledge, or ability to convey what the role of Black fathers means to Black women. The journey with my own father is such a complicated yet simple one. My father tends to exist on the fringes of my life. He is there. He is not there. He is absent but constant. He is my dad, but not my daddy. I often experience a pang of jealousy whenever I hear women refer to their fathers as "my daddy." I believe they have experienced a familiarity with their fathers that I haven't. A familiarity that they will always be "daddy's little girl." They have a surety that he will show up to all major life events and he will bear witness to their lives in a meaningful and rewarding way. I have a cousin who is 50 years old and still refers to her father as "Daddy." She and her father have an undeniable bond, and when I'm around them, I realize how much I missed. Her father is currently experiencing some health problems, but his eyes still light up when she enters the room. I can literally see her transform into a little girl in his presence. They have a playful, easy interaction. They have a knowledge of each other, a history. It is something that I didn't have. My father was 18 years old when he got my 17-year-old mother pregnant. The reality of how young my parents were never fully hit me until I was in the adoption process and the adoption agency connected us to a 17-year-old who was pregnant by her 18-year-old boyfriend. When they sent pictures of this young couple who were the parents of our potential baby, I was shocked. They were babies themselves having babies. And I couldn't help but think they were the same age as my parents when they chose to have me. The young boy seemed to be playing dress up in clothes that were several sizes too big for him. He displayed a sense of bravado that seemed like he was desperately trying to hide his insecurities. He looked defiantly into the camera, and all I could see was a frightened little Black boy trying his best to be a man in a world that didn't see him.

As I looked at him, I thought about my father. How he must have tried to bravely exert himself and look after his new family. How did he deal with the domineering personalities of my two grandmothers? My father was definitely a mama's boy, and my earliest memories of my dad involve him leaving the apartment he shared with my mother and taking me with him to his mother's house every Saturday to vacuum and dust her house. We would spend the entire day there and not leave until the evening. And I now wonder what my mother thought of this peculiar Saturday ritual that my father had with his mother. As a child, he would read the newspaper at the dinner table every night, and I remember him handing me the paper so my five-year-old self could read it. He expressed delight at having such a smart daughter who could read the paper.

My final childhood memory of my father is when I was 12 and my brother was 6. We are in England on our way to the airport to fly to Canada. We are in the car, and my father is crying. My parents have split up. My mother is now in Canada and she has requested that my father send "her children" to her. My father is raging through his tears. He cannot believe that my mother has chosen to walk away from her family. He does not want to send us to our mother, but he feels he has no choice. I am unsure what to do with this unusual display of emotion, so I say nothing.

I am thankful that when we arrived at the security gates to board our plane, my father handed me a copy of *The Color Purple* to read during the flight. It is the first book that I would ever read that featured a Black protagonist, so I was excited. In my excitement, I overlooked my father's pain. The pain of losing his two children, who will now be oceans away. I often wondered why he agreed to send us to go live with my mother. Why didn't he fight for his children? The biggest thing I continue to ponder is: If I grew up with the belief that my father fought for us, truly fought for me, and chose me time and time again, would that have changed my promiscuous teen years where I continued to pick boyfriends and men who obviously didn't choose me? I think about what it would have been like to have a strong, healthy display of manhood in our home, and what influence that might have had on my life. Would I walk through the world differently?

And I know I'm not alone. Many of my clients search back over the histories of their lives and find that the relationship they have or did not have with their fathers has a direct impact on what partners they chose in their lives. You only have to watch one episode of *Iyanla, Fix My Life* to see many of us are suffering from major daddy issues.

Girl, do you have daddy issues? Doing the work that I do and talking to thousands of women, I usually find that most women pick a variation of the following men.

YOUR MAN HAS A WIFE AND A GIRLFRIEND!

Yes, I have read the stats, and I'm aware of the so-called news that apparently there is a man shortage. I have heard many sisters declare, "All the good ones are either married, in jail, or gay!" But, sis, that doesn't give you the right to lay up with someone's husband. You deserve someone who is going to be there for you. You deserve to not be the side chick. I once had a friend who would take pictures of her delicious drinks and fancy meals and post them on Facebook. These were dinners set for two, but there she was smiling alone, and what was noticeably absent was her dinner companion. He would never appear. And I knew it was because he was married. It was very symbolic that it was obvious something or someone was missing—because I would often wonder what was missing within her that she thought this should be enough for her.

I also had a client who spent 10 years of her life with a married man. She told no one. Even her closest friends just thought she was this career-driven woman who had no time for dating. He was her boss, and he promised for years that he would leave his wife, but he always had an excuse. He also "borrowed" large sums of money from her that he never repaid. Keeping this secret and lying to her friends and family for years took a toll on her. She looked years older, her hair had begun to thin, and she felt weighed down and tired. She was absolutely miserable. After consulting with me and also doing some intense sessions with a licensed therapist, she finally found the courage to leave him. I worked with her to gain clarity about what she was looking for in a partner. I encouraged her to try online dating. We met weekly to evaluate if she was picking suitable men who shared her values. Within a few weeks of being online, she went on several dates, and soon met an amazing man who didn't hesitate to put a ring on it. They are now married with two amazing children. The changes in my client are remarkable. She looks years younger, she is happy, and she finally left her job and is now living the life she truly deserves, no longer waiting on someone who had no intention of choosing her.

Sis, the chances of your married man leaving his wife for you are slim to none. And yes, I know there are only a few cases that debunk this theory. But, girl, how you got him is how you will lose him! Do you really want to be the mistress who got the guy in the end? You deserve more. You deserve a love that picks you from the beginning. A love that is able to show up for you at all times. A love that is rooted in progress and growth, not false hope and promises. Maybe you had a mother who dated several married men, and this situation reminds you of her. Or maybe you had a mother who often declared, "Men ain't shit!" So you think you shouldn't expect much from a man and you keep picking men who cannot be there for you. Sis, you already know, someone else's husband cannot give you the love you truly desire. Sis, let him go!

FALLING IN LOVE WITH HIS POTENTIAL

You're a superstar! You have your shit together. You're killing it at work. The world is your oyster. You have a well-rounded life, great friends, a career you love, a beautiful home . . . And laid up on your couch playing Xbox is your man! He's been there all day while you've been at work. And you are fully committed to supporting him through the rough patch he's been going through for the last three years! Girl, you know he ain't shit, but you keep trying. You proofread his resume; damn, girl, you even typed it up for him. You sat for hours with him, sending it out to various places online. But somehow, after landing the interview and getting the job, it doesn't work out. Maybe it's because he slept through the alarm one too many times. And there he is back on your couch. But you know he has the potential to do big things with his life. You know this because you are now helping him put his business plan together. This guy has dreams. And of course the sex is amazing! Mr. Xbox knows how to blow your back out. So, you keep hope alive because that "D" is something special.

Maybe he reminds you of your broken and bitter daddy, who was at the dinner table every night lamenting that "Black men never get a break. Someone always trying to hold them back."

So you want to prove to your man that you will hold him down to the bitter end. But this ain't your daddy and, sis, you know it's time to let it go. Meet him where he is. Not where you want him to be. Someone needs to add to your life, not subtract from it. In one of my favorite songs,

"Add to Me," by R&B singing sensation, Ledisi, she asks any potential suitors how they are going to make her life better because her life is already good. Be like Ledisi, sis, and ask those questions. Because it is not your job to take care of a man! Both of you need to support each other. Be able to build together. And no matter how good the sex is, you deserve something more. Sis, let it go!

THE MAN-CHILD

Unfortunately, this is the one I see many of us end up marrying! We tell ourselves it's better to have someone than no one. He is immature. Usually, he just left his mama's house so he could walk you down the aisle. His mama comes first, his boyz second, his car third, and then you. You usually spend most of your relationship giving him basic instructions on how to get through life—things such as when the dishwasher is full, push this button to turn it on! Or the garbage is overflowing so can you please take it out and yes, you need to replace the bag!

And you are okay with being his mama until you have kids of your own, and then you realize that you don't have the time or energy to look after a grown-ass man plus children who actually need you. But now you're stuck. You know you have a man-child and not a true partner you can count on. But you stick it out because, hell, at least you got a man! Maybe your marriage reminds you of your parents—your mother arguing with your daddy to help her around the house, and your daddy responding by turning up the TV!

Sis, you deserve more.

MR. EMOTIONALLY UNAVAILABLE

He's tall, good looking, has a great job, an amazing body. He's got money and great credit. You can bring him to all your work events, and he won't embarrass you. He's charming, intelligent, and probably went to Howard University, FAMU, or Morehouse. He's that Black dude. And you love to show him off. He gets you wet just by sending a "Goodnight, beautiful" text, and then you don't hear from him for weeks. You can see he's reading all your texts, but he just never responds.

So you play detective just to reassure yourself that he's alive! You search his social media for clues, notice that he recently changed his profile picture, and you see that he has liked several of his friends' comments; even had the nerve to write something on some skanky girl's picture. But he can't call you back? But all is forgiven when he sends flowers to you at work and finally calls you and tells you that he misses you and work has been a nightmare, and he would love to take you out for dinner. You agree and put on your Beyoncé freakum dress. He picks you up in his drop-top BMW. At dinner, he can't take his eyes off you. You build up the nerve to ask him, "Where do you see this going?" He smoothly replies, "Girl, you know I got you."

You know you deserve more, but somehow you end up back at his house, your panties on the floor. Two weeks later, and you're still waiting for him to text you back! Maybe, deep down, it reminds you of the time when your dad said he was going to pick you up, and you put on your favorite dress, and your momma combed your hair while you waited patiently by the door, and he never showed up.

Sis, you need a love that is going to choose you and claim you at all times. You need a love that is going to show up.

We are all products of our environment. Somehow we get stuck in the narratives of our childhood and try to fix what was missing as a child in our adulthood.

I'm excited about the examples of celebrity women who have publicly leveled up and gotten rid of the men who were clearly wasting their time. We all cheered for Ciara when she moved on from Future and his 10,000 baby mothers and found her a man who clearly adored her and her son. It was obvious that Ciara had a penchant for "bad boy" rappers. And she has stated that it was only after the birth of her child that she knew she had to do something differently. She wanted something more for herself. She often talks about the prayer she made to bring a man like Russell into her life. It was a prayer of intention, a prayer of clarity. She became a woman very clear on what she brought to the table and was no longer settling for less.

And of course, we cheer double-time for Cassie, who spent 10 years with Diddy! No ring, no marriage, just being some fancy arm candy. Diddy seemed content to keep the status quo. And when Cassie jumped ship and started posting pictures of her personal trainer, who claimed her, married her, and started a family with her within months of dating. . . We all knew that Cassie was a woman who wasn't about the fame or the money but about having someone love her properly and give her the love that she truly deserved.

And I don't know the daddy stories of these women, but what I do know is something clicked and they realized that they were allowing the mistreatment. They were accepting less than their worth. And people treat you the way you allow them to treat you. So, sis, is it time for you to level up? Is it time to write your own Ciara prayer or keep it moving like Cassie?

For myself, I used to think that having an emotionally absent father didn't affect me, but it did. I chose partners who did not give to me emotionally. I was often left emotionally drained because I was giving so much and not getting it back in return. I never traced it back to my father until I did some deep soul healing work that involved intense therapy, healing of my inner child, and intentionally trying to establish a connection with my father. Recently, my father became ill, and during his initial treatment, we became closer as I helped him decide what course of treatment he needed. I'm not sure if it was because he was now facing his own mortality, but my father became softer, less private, and for the first time, he initiated a conversation and picked up the phone more often.

As I wrote this chapter, I realized there was so much about my father that I didn't know. So I came up with an elaborate story about writing a book about Black women and their fathers and told him that I wanted to talk to him about his life. My father was resistant at first. He expressed that he had nothing much to talk about. But he eventually agreed to talk with me via phone every Saturday at 3 P.M. A couple of hours before our planned phone calls, I would send my father a few questions. Some of them were mundane—about his favorite meal and favorite color. Others went deeper as I inquired about his childhood and lessons he learned about love. During our first call my father was guarded and tried to rush me off the phone, declaring, "This is a load of rubbish!" But by our second call, he could barely contain his excitement as he reminisced about his childhood, his dreams, his life. I couldn't get a word in as he talked about his first love, his dreams as a young boy, his mother and grandmother, his best friends, the first car he bought, the girl who broke his heart . . . He started to look forward to our calls and sometimes afterward he would send me a text with things he forgot to mention. Our calls gave me a glimpse into a man that I realized I really didn't know. I was amazed by his thoughts, his dreams, and his beliefs, and as he shared many things from his challenging childhood, I realized he had never been given permission to fully express himself or to have his experiences validated. I loved those talks and over the course of six weeks of calls I learned so much. I realized that I not only loved this man but had grown to really like him. He finally had let me in. There is still work that needs to be done, but as I learned more about my father I become softer and more forgiving with myself, and I now extend that courtesy to my father. I remember that he was a child having a child when he had me. Just like me, he is now doing the best that he can. I saw my father. I saw my dad. I found my daddy.

SIS, GET YOUR MIND RIGHT!

1. Write a letter of forgiveness to your father. In it, describe all the ways he let you down as well as what and who you wanted and needed him to be. Include things that he did as you were growing up that showed you that he loved you and cared. End the letter by stating, "I'm no longer a child, so I love you and release you. I will be in charge of parenting myself now."

2. Take an honest and deep look at your current and past relationships. Do any of the descriptions of the various types of men resonate with you? What does a healthy relationship look like to you? What does an emotionally available partner look like?

3. If you see a pattern in terms of picking men who do not pick you, sis, seek out therapy, or invest in a good relationship or lifestyle coach. You must get committed to healing the wounds of your childhood and examining the relationship you had or have with your father.

affirmations

I CHOOSE A HEALTHY BIG LOVE AND
THE SAME CHOOSES ME.

I'M EXCITED THAT MY LOVE HAS FOUND ME.

LOVE SHOWS UP IN MY LIFE IN THE MOST
BEAUTIFUL AND PROFOUND WAYS.

chapter 15

Sis, Who Hurt You?

Black Girl Playlist:
"Bag Lady,"
Erykah Badu

When I'm scared, frightened, lonely, or feeling aban-
doned, I make space for that little girl who I know dwells
inside me. I no longer ignore her. I know that she is here.
I know she is waiting for me to mother her. Mother her
in the ways that the adults in my life were ill-equipped
to do. I also understand that the adults, including my
grandmothers and mother, did the best they could. Many
of them were mothering under less-than-ideal circumstances, yet society had placed so many unrealistic expectations on them and their children. I recently read this
quote on the Instagram page of Black Women in Motion:

"There's a lot to unpack about the heavy expectations
levied on Black womxn. They are the only flowers that are
expected to blossom despite not being watered."

Those words left me speechless, weary, and emotional. As a child, I expected the women in my life to adequately mother me, but many of them were not being watered. As Black children, we should not have had to bear the consequences of this lack of water, but many of us do and did.

We know about the tough, no-nonsense Black mother. She is mothering under less-than-ideal circumstances. She is overwhelmed, and her feelings of helplessness are often taken out on her children's young spirits and minds. Both my brother and I have borne the brunt physically and emotionally of my mother's feelings of being overwhelmed. My mother has also recalled childhood beatings by my grandmother that were questionable in their viciousness. Often, my mother didn't think the punishment fit the crime. Yet the cycle was repeated with her children. And many of my clients share the same story of severe punishment doled out by their mothers. Mothers who were tired, overwhelmed, and under-resourced. Those physical assaults on their children's bodies were the only way that some mothers may have felt they could assert any sort of control over their lives. Many of us are connected by our collective pain of what discipline looked like in our household. We all know that Black mommas don't play and their threat to beat you into next week is a real one. And sometimes when I'm out shopping, I will witness a frustrated, tired mother out with her kids, and she is blunt and harsh with them. She does not seem kind or patient. As Black mothers, some of us seem to continue the harsh disciplinary actions of our mothers, and it is time we reexamine that. We must stay committed to ending the generational trauma and abuse that has occurred in some of our families.

Usually when I'm holding my son, I will kiss him and tell him I love him. I'm very aware of the tone I use to speak to him. I want him to know that he deserves softness and kindness, and I want him to expect that he will receive these things from his mother. I do not believe I have to be harsh or cruel to prepare him for the hardness I know will come when eventually he grows up to be a Black man in a world that does not have the reputation of responding to him kindly. Often, I am cautioned by my mother and other family members that I'm spoiling him. Too much love, too much of me holding him, immediately going to him when he's crying, will spoil him. We need to look at the messaging we receive as Black mothers and perhaps change the narrative.

And I know my mother genuinely believes that if she wasn't hard on us we would not be the success stories that we are today. And yes that is partly true, but that is not the full picture. I needed and desired a softer mother. A mother who could hold space for that little girl who was me. Yet as she ages my mother has changed her approach to parenting. She has become kinder and softer. She often expresses that she doesn't want to have the relationship with her children that my grandmother had with her. And when I think about my mother I often reflect on the Maya Angelou quote, "When you know better, you do better." My mother has been committed to doing better and has clearly evolved as a parent. Therefore, I try to parent by taking the best things from her but also examining what didn't work. And for us to end generational trauma and abuse, we must be able to take stock of what worked and what beliefs and attitudes perpetuate cycles of abuse in our community, homes, and lives.

Yet I am my mother's child. My sister, who has a closer relationship with our mother than I do, expressed that the reason my mother and I have experienced so much conflict in our earlier years is that we are so similar. It is true. Both of us have a tell-like-it-is approach. We are known to have little to no filter. We are both bossy and think our way is the best. We can be stubborn. We both enjoy watching *Dateline* and *20/20*, and there isn't a crime story that doesn't have us mesmerized. We also love people and we love to talk to strangers, make new friends, host people, and gather people together. We have a love of comedy and we love laughing at ourselves and we love when the joke is on us! We are also tenderhearted. Give us a sob story and we are there to help.

Years ago a young Black Jamaican man came to our door selling vacuums. During the presentation, he shared with my mother that he was homeless, he was in the country illegally, and he had nowhere to go. My mother, without hesitation, offered him a home with us. He moved in, and overnight we became family. "Uncle Leroy" became my mother's little brother. He stayed with us for about a year until he got back on his feet. During this time, my mother helped him find a job, clothed and fed him, and helped him with his immigration. Years later when I asked her why she helped him, she said, "Trey, always remember, everyone is somebody's child. I give grace to other people's children because I hope someone will offer you grace when I'm not there." It is a lesson that has stayed with me my entire life. When it is possible, offer someone grace.

And that is my mother. She's known to go to the food bank to pick up food for her elderly neighbors and distributed it as if she's Robin Hood. She will pick up old people waiting at the bus stop and drop them wherever they need to go. And she will literally give you the shirt off her back. Similar to my mother, I have been known to take homeless people to my home for a meal and or bring them to a shelter or pick up people at the bus stop if it's cold and drive them to where they are going. As my brother cautions, "You love a broken bird and you need to be careful."

But alongside our kindness and generosity, my mother and I are both known for our hot tempers, and we are the first to put you in check if you try to come for us or our family!

So I know there is a softness with my mother, a kindness to strangers, but there is also a woman who has challenges with being soft to her children. When I first watched *The Cosby Show*, Clair Huxtable gave to me a different idea of motherhood. Here was a woman who spoke to her children calmly, who was a firm disciplinarian, but also created an environment where her children could be seen and heard. And yes, she was a fictional character; however, here she was in the mainstream media giving us Black motherhood reimagined. We need to reimagine motherhood and who we want or need to be. We need to think about our own healing in motherhood. You may already be a mother. Or you are thinking of motherhood. Or perhaps you are experiencing infertility, or maybe you have decided that motherhood isn't for you. Either way, this is a chance to look at the messaging we have received about motherhood. Studies have shown that we tend to model the parenting practices of our own childhood. When I was younger and thinking about parenting, I could not conceive of parenting that did not involve a good ass whooping for my misbehaving children. That is how I was raised, so I thought that was what I should do. Now that I have been exposed to other ideas of parenting and I have also been exposed to adults who did not receive the harsh disciplinary traumas I did, I know that I will not use corporal punishment with my children.

If a child is not traumatized in their own home, perhaps when they reach adulthood, they would not be open to someone treating them unkindly in their own home. What if we as Black women started to teach young Black girls that it is unacceptable for someone to afflict physical pain on their young bodies? I often wonder who we would be then. Would we be softer, more vulnerable, more trusting because we are used to be handled in ways that feel kinder and more loving? Would we parent differently if trauma wasn't our biggest resource? How would some of us parent if our mothers and fathers had shown up in ways that mirrored healing, love, acceptance, security, and kindness?

We can change the cycle and dynamics of our families. Change starts with us.

SIS, GET YOUR MIND RIGHT!

1. Write down the ways as a child you were disciplined.

2. How would you have liked discipline to look like as a child?

3. Write a letter to your inner child and describe how you will protect her from future harm and hurt. Tell her how you will emotionally keep her safe.

4. If you are a parent are there things that you wish to change or shift in your approach to parenting and discipline?

affirmations

I LOVE AND FORGIVE MY MOTHER.

ALL UNHEALTHY DYNAMICS WITHIN
MY FAMILY END WITH ME.

I SHOW UP TO MY LIFE FULLY
HEALED, LOVED, AND HEALTHY.

chapter 16

Beautiful Black Girl

BLACK GIRL PLAYLIST:
"BROWN SKIN GIRL,"
BEYONCÉ

"I think it pisses God off if you walk by the color purple in a field somewhere and don't notice it. People think pleasing God is all God cares about. But any fool living in the world can see it always trying to please us back."

—ALICE WALKER, *THE COLOR PURPLE*

Sometimes, we are so busy that we walk by the beauty in our lives—we are oblivious to all of it. And the beauty we miss happens in so many ways.

If you're a type A personality like me, you know that many times we are so focused on the future and where we need to be that we miss the beauty of today. We have become so jaded that we miss the everyday moments of awe. Children have a way of reminding us to be in that moment. I love seeing the world through my son's eyes, how everything is a new experience for him. My son was six months old when—exhausted—I decided to kill two birds with one stone and hop in the shower with him so I could shower and also bathe him at the same time. What I wasn't expecting was his joy and awe at the water spouting from the shower head. His delightful giggles as the water hit his skin. I had taken all these moments for granted and I was overcome with emotion as I watched him feel all these new sensations for the first time. And it's the simple things, such as his fascination with the ceiling fan, how he smiles at me when I sing along to a song on the radio, or how his wide eyes fill with glee that remind me that he is present with me in this very moment. Many times, we miss the moment because we are going over our long to-do lists. We are worried that it won't last, so we are already thinking of what it will feel like when it's past. We need to remind ourselves that all we have is right here. Writing this book during a pandemic is a clear reminder of that. All of a sudden, the world as we knew it stopped. We were not prepared. We did not know from one day to the next how drastically our lives could change. We took every day as it came, thankful that it was here. We got rid of outside distractions and found joy in simplicity. We now had time to slow down and take in every moment. We no longer took our families for granted. We were painfully aware that death could be around the corner because we saw healthy people perishing, making us live in the moment and be thankful that each day we were given the gift of life.

I implore you to live in the moment. One of my favorite quotes is from Mother Teresa, and I have it illustrated on my living room wall to remind me to slow down and be in the moment:

"Yesterday is gone, tomorrow has not yet come. We only have today. Let us begin."

Sis, live for today. Do not let the beauty of the present moment pass you by. Slow down.

BEAUTY IN PEOPLE

Several times when I'm working with women and they talk about what they are looking for in a relationship, they will start with a list of physical attributes the potential partner has to meet. Many women will turn down potential partners if they are wearing the wrong color shoes. I once worked with a successful doctor who was an empty nester. She was beautiful, smart, and had everything going for her, but she couldn't figure out why she was single and couldn't meet the right guy. I wasn't quite sure either why love had alluded her until our next session when she shared that she had recently gone on a fabulous date with a man who was smart, caring, emotionally available, and who called her after their date to set up the second one. The second date was also great. But after date number three, she was disillusioned. This wasn't the guy for her. Why? Her date had made the grave mistake of wearing the same shirt he wore on date number one to their third date! She had decided that this meant he wasn't a person who would put in any effort for her. And she told him so, stating that she expected a bit more effort! She couldn't understand why he ghosted her after that conversation! After all, she was just being honest and wanted him to know that she expected him to put more effort into his clothing. She had focused on his clothing and overlooked all the wonderful things he brought to the table. It may sound absurd, but how often have we overlooked inner beauty because the package outside didn't match what we thought we would be attracted to? Take notice of the inner beauty of people. Appreciate people for who they truly are.

MAKING OURSELVES BEAUTIFUL

In our interview, Dr. LaShawnDa Pittman shared that during slavery, Black women who had spent hours in the field doing physical labor for masters would also do work for their families as well. They would still make time to attend secret parties, and to get ready for these parties, they would use what little money they had to secretly buy beads, make dye to make colorful clothing, and do whatever they could to beautify their clothes. They were invested in making themselves beautiful. They would also comb their hair into intricate styles to make themselves feel beautiful. They would find beauty in their natural hair. We now see it becoming more popular for Black women to take pride in their natural hair and wear it in its natural state. She stated, "Black people and especially Black women are the only group where they have tried to legislate how we look . . . These different governments, employers, and companies are trying to tell us how we can wear our hair! And I don't think it's because they find it unattractive. It is because they know it's empowering for us to feel beautiful, attractive, and to walk in our natural beauty. Doing so affirms Black is beautiful. And a beautiful, empowered Black woman is a threat. So they try to rob us of our natural inclination and desire to feel beautiful in our own skin and with our hair."

We need to remind ourselves of our beauty. We need to take time to find the beauty in our natural state. My mother began perming my hair at age four, so I had no

idea what my natural hair looked like. When I began loc-
ing my hair, my mother and grandmother voiced numerous concerns about the "unprofessional look" of locs. They
worried about how the world would perceive me. Yet I
knew I was no longer invested in something that had me
putting chemicals in my hair that burned my scalp and
forced me to live up to a beauty ideal that no longer fit
me. Going natural was empowering for me. I have been
wearing my hair natural for many years, and when my
hair is freshly done, twisted, and oiled, I feel so beautiful.
For me, twisting and combing my hair is the way I bring
beauty and beauty rituals into my life. As Black women,
we need to take the time to figure out how to beautify ourselves. For some, it may mean perming or adding exten-
sions and a weave. For some, it is rocking a short natural
fade. Whatever it is, we must find beauty in ourselves. We
must be able to look back at the girl in the mirror and
fall in love with her daily. We also must remember that
other little Black girls are watching us. They know what
we place value on. In a popular think piece I wrote for the
Huffington Post called "State of Emergency for Black Girls,"
I shared the following:

"*Lately, I've become overly aware of little Black girls
between the ages of six to eleven years old. Little Black girls
with thick, short or long braids. Sometimes in their hair, they
have a dozen rainbow colorful clips or multicolored beads, or
tiny braids cane-rowed tightly into beautiful masterpieces.
Their hair parted four million little ways with heavily greased
scalps. They have thick beautiful lips, flat cute noses, and soul-
ful big eyes. Their chocolate brown skin glistening, yet often
they have forgotten to lotion ashy elbows or knees.*

"*These little Black girls remind me of myself. And I look
for me in them, searching to find myself. When our eyes meet,*

I smile; if they smile back, I often compliment them on their beautiful hair or tell them what a pretty smile they have. Mostly they seem shocked that someone has even acknowledged them, much less dared to call them beautiful! And the darker their skin, and the thicker or shorter their hair, the more shocked they seem that someone has called them beautiful. They coyly look away, and I know that they are questioning if I am indeed telling them the truth. Is it possible? Are they really beautiful?

"In their various shapes, sizes and shades that range from cinnamon brown to blue black, I loudly declare and express how beautiful they are. I tell them that they are beautiful because I vividly remember when I was their age how I wanted someone to call me pretty, or beautiful."

We must be able to find the beauty in ourselves but also remind our daughters, our sisters, our nieces, and all little Black girls that they are beautiful because the messaging that they get is that they are not beautiful. So, we must remind ourselves of our beauty, empower each other, and serve as beautiful role models.

BEAUTIFYING OUR HOME

As a child, there was a lot of movement and transition in my life. Lots of instability. I have clear memories of my brother and me packing up our stuff in plastic bags to be moved again. Many times, we were given only a few hours' notice, and from day to day, our living situation could change at any given time. As a child, I lived with my maternal grandmother, then my parents, then my paternal grandmother, then my maternal grandmother, and then my mother, then back to my maternal grandmother, and finally back with my mother and stepfather, and eventually, I was kicked out of the house at age 19. I even spent some time in a youth shelter. So it was no wonder that I had a hard time as an adult creating permanency in my home. As an adult, I moved several times. There was one year where I moved four times!

I had stuff in storage. Stuff at friends' places. Stuff at exes' places. Most of my belongings had a home at numerous spots. Each of my apartments felt like I was squatting. I would never fully unpack. Even when I bought my first home. I quickly got roommates and allowed them to take over the decor of the home and gave them permission to do what they pleased to make the house a home. I moved most of my belongings into the basement, and they stayed there for several years. Upstairs I lived in sparse surroundings, using my roommates' furniture and a few selected items. I never quite trusted that I would stay long enough anywhere to make it a home.

I had a core belief that I did not need a home. I did not want to create an attachment to anything. It wasn't until I moved to Atlanta and bought my dream home that I started to really examine how and why I went my entire life not creating a true home for myself. Several of my exes commented on my ability to create "home" using a small corner space in their apartments, never quite settling, and my resistance to committing to build a home and a life with them. I was scared about making a home with someone in case they would tell me to leave, so I had a transient mindset. I didn't feel that I would be too long at any given space. Also I was known to carry more than the average person would in my knapsack. I said it was part of my OCD to have a toothbrush, underwear, and change of clothes in a knapsack at all times, but I also knew it was also deeply rooted in fear, so if the need arose, I would have enough at any moment to flee a situation. And yes, it was a running joke to many, but I knew there was more to this.

My therapist worked with me to examine my resistance around planting roots. Diving into the emotional pain of an unstable childhood and what home meant or didn't mean to me, I was given painstaking instructions by my therapist that I was to make my house a home. That included unpacking every box—I was not allowed to put an unopened box in the basement. I wasn't allowed to hire any help such as an interior designer or organizer. I needed to figure out what drawer I wanted my knives and forks to go into. I also had to paint the home with the colors that I liked. And the hardest tasks I was given were to pick pictures—family pictures—frame them, and put them up, and also select and buy personal art to put up. At first, I was overwhelmed by the prospect of finally creating a home in my mid-thirties, but I knew it was the only way I could fully address the childhood trauma of insecurity and unsettlement in my life.

Once I got started, I began to truly enjoy the process of beautifying my home. From picking plants and scented candles to painting murals on the walls and framing inspirational quotes, I started to enjoy personalizing my space. This was the first time that I had ever lived alone, and for once, I didn't have to consult with anyone. I could do whatever I wanted. By the time the house was finished, I realized I had a unique, untapped talent and ability to put colors and pieces together. Friends were in awe of the beauty of my home; many of them requested that I go shopping with them to help design their homes. And I had fallen in love with my own space. My home became my sanctuary. I loved coming home after being on tour for several months or turning my key in the door after an extremely long day. I loved seeing pictures of Black women and my favorite quotes on my wall, eating from my favorite colorful plates that I had bought from a local potter—all these things made my home beautiful. And I realized how important it is for us as Black women to create beautiful spaces. It doesn't matter what size your home is. It could be a simple room, a studio apartment, or a sprawling mini mansion. What's important is that we must make our homes beautiful. We must believe we are deserving of beauty and not wait for the perfect time or the perfect mate to create a beautiful home. As a Black Girl in love (with yourself), you deserve a space to claim as truly yours. As I mentioned in an earlier chapter, decluttering and getting rid of junk is important. Pia Overjoy, an amazing Black woman who is the owner of Sweet Digs, a home organizing consulting business, helps women turn their houses into beautiful spaces that reflect their true sense of self and purpose. She recommends on her Instagram that you "change your mindset and comfortably keep what sparks joy and discard the rest so you will have lasting change."

SIS, GET YOUR MIND RIGHT!

1. Take a look at your current living environment. Does your home reflect beauty? Does it make you feel happy? Is it a true reflection of you?

2. What small project could you take on to beautify your home? Get your pictures framed? Declutter your kitchen?

3. Whose home have you recently gone in or seen that you admire? What did you like about their home that you can now incorporate into your own?

affirmations

I AM LIVING IN MY BEAUTIFUL DREAM HOME.

MY HOME IS SAFE, PEACEFUL, AND FILLED WITH LOVE.

I REALLY ENJOY LIVING IN AN ORGANIZED
AND UNCLUTTERED HOME.

epilogue

This Black Girl Is Definitely in Love (with Herself)

BLACK GIRL PLAYLIST: "WALKING TROPHY," HOODCELEBRITYY

"I wouldn't take nothing for my journey now," is one of my favorite quotes from Maya Angelou. It reminds me that everything, every single moment, good or bad, was orchestrated by the Universe for you to learn something about yourself. Some of these lessons literally left me on my knees in a stand-up shower. Some have left me on the bathroom floor in a fetal position. And some broke my heart, and I had to painstakingly be tender and kind to myself as I searched for all the pieces to try to patch myself together. Some moments left me breathless, breathless with joy. Some moments have left me giddy. Some have left me raising my hands to the sky in joy. This has been a journey like no other. I have danced like no one is watching. I have been brave. I have also been scared. Scared to use my own voice. Scared to ask for what I know I deserved. I have sat in a room full of people and experienced aching loneliness, and I have been alone in my room full of hope and wonder while truly feeling the divine spirit of the Universe. I have laughed. Girl, I have deep-belly laughed as tears rolled down my face. And I have laughed during some very inappropriate times. I have given a friend a secret look from across the room, and we have both burst into uncontrollable laughter. Laughter has gotten me through so many good and bad times.

And my friends. My amazing friends have seen me through so much. They have been my cheerleaders, the people who have fed me emotionally with big plates of overflowing food. They have been the ones to take my phone and delete all my pictures of my ex. They have been the ones to remind me that I deserve so much more. They have been my hype women. My friends have surrounded me like mama bears and praying grandmas, knowing they needed to hold me down in my weakest hours. And they have borne witness to some of the foolishness I have done in the name of love and have encouraged me to call them no matter what time instead of making a damn fool of myself! And when I find myself in some place or position that is not worthy of my time, effort, or presence, we have laughed at my antics, which has helped me to not judge myself so harshly.

I'm glad I come from a family who doesn't take themselves too seriously and taught me that the best jokes are when the joke is on you. My family, in all their dysfunction, are the ones I know will show up. They will be there. We will argue and we will fight, but we are fierce with our loyalty. You come for one of us, you come for all of us. I have a mother who leads with kindness and generosity. She has shown me that no matter how little you have there is always enough to share with someone else. My mother is a living, breathing example of falling down, getting back up, falling down, and getting back up again. She's a fighter, and I could never be anyone but her tell-it-like-it-is daughter who is brave even when she's scared. My mother—who doesn't allow me to take myself too seriously, no matter how many venues I pack and how many awards I win—will be the first one to laugh at my no-rhythm-self dancing on stage. And lately, the Universe has been showing me not to take myself too seriously because the Universe has a great way of making you fall flat on your face, and when you do, the only way you can get up is to have a true sense of humor.

I have a grandmother whose spirit I feel every day guiding me, whispering to me. She is in heaven orchestrating for all types of blessings and good fortune to come my way. She is the voice I hear when someone's inability to love me right makes me question if I'm indeed "special." I hear her screaming at me, "Gyal, you are special, don't mek anybody tek you for no damn fool! Love your damn self! You are born with luck!" My granny is the example of making a way when you think there is no way.

I have a dad who is a reminder that sometimes you need to be quiet and just listen. You need to observe what is going on. You don't always have to have the loudest voice in the room or take up the most space. Sometimes it is enough to just be in the room. His love is quiet and constant. It is a love that I can always count on.

But I now know that the type A, super anal me can plan and create the most detailed map of my life, yet the Universe may give me an unexpected plot twist that not even badass Shonda Rhimes could have written. Those plot twists have shown me I'm stronger than I know, and I must have faith it will all make sense in the end. And even when it doesn't, it's a lesson in learning to just let shit go! It has also shown me that my friends and loved ones will show up for me as I try to figure out what the next chapter of my life needs to be. I also know that no one owes you an explanation for why they stopped loving you. And yes, it will hurt. It will hurt like hell. But the only way you will truly heal is if you have enough love for yourself. And if you understand that you didn't give them the job of loving you—while they were loving you, you were also busy loving yourself! And most importantly, you must know how to love yourself when they are gone. Never give away the power to love yourself. Or love yourself correctly. Teach people how to love you.

And, sis, if I have learned anything, it is to release yourself from those pressing timelines that you have planned. I remember being 16 years old and singing along with Luther Vandross as my best friend and I practiced our wedding march in my bedroom. We were certain that I would marry the pimply-faced teenage boy who just felt up my boobs in the back of his dad's car. We would buy houses next door to each other, and our kids would be best friends, and . . . The unrealistic dream just never happened. And maybe the timeline has been tweaked from your 16-year-old self, but many of us are still invested in the timeline that included:

- Meeting "your person" by 25
- Having the wedding of your dreams by 27

- Buying a house with your person at 30
- Having kids by 32
- . . . and, well, you know the rest.

When we don't meet those milestones, we feel as though we have severely failed in life. We get panicked, so we come down harder on ourselves. Or, to meet those milestones, we stay in shit that we had no business being in. Or we stare longingly at the timelines of others who are living our so-called dream life. And we feel like bigger pieces of shit for not living up to those unrealistic timelines. When my whole life unceremoniously blew up in my face, I sat with shame for months, thinking I had failed. Failed at having someone choose me and failed at not being able to post #couplegoals. I had failed at not being able to provide my son with a family unit. I had failed at life because someone did not choose to love me forever. As my mother graciously put it, even though no one had damn well asked her, "Trey, it's so sad that this is where you are at this time in your life." I felt as though someone had punched me in the gut. And, for months, I thought she was right, that my life had no meaning because here I was in my forties with no one choosing me. I wallowed in self-pity. I sat with the thoughts that something must truly be wrong with me, that someone could just up and walk out of my life without even a backward glance. Every single abandonment issue came up for me. Every single childhood trauma was activated, and I had no sense of what I needed to do to stop feeling like a failure. Until one day, while journaling, I got a clear message from the Universe: "Girl, choose yourself." And I knew that was indeed the simple answer. I couldn't expect anyone to choose me if I had not chosen myself first. So I intentionally started to choose myself daily, and I started to be softer and kinder to that little girl in me who was begging to be chosen.

Funny enough, my son became the direct living replica of how I wanted to speak to that scared little girl that dwelled inside of me. When I was soft and gentle with him and encouraging him, I spoke to myself in that same voice that I used to soothe or encourage him. Whenever I felt "Critical Cathy" losing her mind, I would shut her up and say, "We no longer speak to Trey like that." And I started to focus on what was working in my life. What things I excelled at and continue to excel at. I started to focus on friends and family who chose me daily. And yes, maybe the person who I thought was my big love walked out on me, but it was a lesson in never expecting someone to love you more than you love yourself.

Months before my life blew up in my face, my shoulder-length locs, which have always been my pride and joy, started to split in the middle. They would break off and I would find pieces of my weak hair in my bed or scattered throughout my fancy apartment. This was truly distressing for me, and I couldn't figure out why this was happening. Also, my favorite plant, which I had carried around from home to home and which now stood nearly four feet tall, just stopped growing. I would water it, and I even repotted it, and it would not grow. This plant had always grown and loved the light and water, but now it remained unmoving, stagnant. Once my relationship ended and I moved into my new home, my hair stopped breaking and just started growing like a weed. The plant magically started producing new leaves and tiny red flowers that I had never seen before. I could not help but think this is symbolic of my journey. My hair will grow when I have emotionally grown. New flowers will bloom when they feel safe. The lesson was, I cannot grow where I do not feel safe, heard, and seen. I cannot grow where I'm not watered. I cannot grow where there is no light. I recently read a post that stated, "Cut off your dead ends for growth and I'm not just talking about your hair."

I couldn't say it any better!

And, girl, the biggest lesson I learned was to stop focusing on what was missing but what was there. I started to find joy. And I sat down with the Universe to ask her what I should do with my newfound knowledge, and it was clear: I was knocked off my high horse to show women that you must get back up. You must find yourself. You must learn to find joy again, and you must fall in love with yourself, time and time again. Loving yourself is not a final destination. You do not get there and it's over. You need to remind yourself daily to be loving and kind. You have to also remind others how to love you. And there are going to be days when you are better at it than others. And there would be days when a small voice, aka Critical Cathy, will pop into your head and try to convince you that you are not worthy of self-love, pleasure, and tenderness—you have to shut that bitch down! Because, sistergirl, you are worthy. You are the BEST!

My favorite dance hall track, which is on repeat in my house nearly every day and truly got me through some of my darkest moments, is "Walking Trophy" by HoodCelebrityy. Why? Because it's a reminder that you need to know that you are a prize! People should be honored to have you in their life! You need to know that you are a big fucking deal! And don't let anyone treat you like you're worth less than you are! You are a damn walking trophy! There is an entire world waiting for your Black girl magic. An entire world waiting for your reinvention of what's next. And you're going to surprise everyone, including your damn self. You are fierce. You are loveable. You are brave. You are intentional. You are beautiful, and, girl, you are loved. You are a Black girl in love with herself!

In my quest to find love, I have failed many times. But I now know that to find true and healthy love, I must first be in love with myself! I also know that being in love with yourself requires firm intentions and actions. So, I have written down a few things that I have learned along the way.

If I were a Black girl in love with myself . . .

I would need to sit alone with myself to know myself. I would know that being alone does not mean being lonely. I would sit with my fears and figure out why I'm afraid of the dark, scared of silence, terrified of having to sit alone with myself.

If I were a Black girl in love with myself . . .

I would choose healthy relationships. One that helps me grow, makes me a better person, feeds and nurtures me. I wouldn't settle for anyone else's husband or man. I wouldn't sign up for partnerships that are physically or emotionally abusive. I would make it clear that I deserve better.

If I were a Black girl in love with myself . . .

I would choose someone who has fully chosen me. Someone who wants to work shit out with me! Someone who desires to wake up with me. Someone who deep-belly laughs with me. I would choose someone who makes my tummy flip, who misses me when I leave the room. Someone who encourages me to be a better and kinder person.

If I were a Black girl in love with myself . . .

I would actively work on being less critical of myself. I would look in the mirror and not wish myself away.

Instead, every day I would loudly declare, "I'm going to take care of you! You are beautiful! I'm proud of you! I love you! I love that kink in your hair, your beautiful nose, your widespread grin, your crooked tooth, that scar on your belly. I would exercise, walk a few steps daily to just honor you! I would not compare you to other women's bodies. I would give thanks to God that he gave me another day with you."

If I were a Black girl in love with myself . . .

I would spend less money on expensive shoes and more money on therapy because I would realize I need to do soul work and not sole work! I need to heal those childhood scars. I need to learn how to forgive all the people who did not do enough to make me feel loved, important, or wanted. Therapy would help me to be okay with asking for what I want from my family, my partnerships, and my friendships. Therapy would help me deal with the depression that often creeps in, leaving me feeling lonely, suicidal, and unworthy.

If I were a Black girl in love with myself . . .

I would take the time to examine my sistah circle. Do my friendships support unhealthy dynamics of petty jealousies, backbiting, and subtle put-downs? Am I everybody's superwoman? Am I always the shoulder to cry on? Am I that "go-to girl" and yet there's no place for me to go to?

If I were a Black girl in love with myself . . .

I would question all the spoken and unspoken "truths" that my mother told me about myself. Did my mother counsel me from a place of fear, anger, hurt, and ignorance? I would lovingly accept that my mother did the best she could, but that doesn't mean her best is now *my* best! I would view my mother in the same loving way I view myself as a person who tries but sometimes fails. I would know that I'm not a replica of my mother or grandmother. I do not have to repeat unhealthy family cycles or dynamics. I would forgive my mother.

If I were a Black girl in love with myself . . .

I would write my father a letter. Mail it to him. Or never mail it. I would tell him all the things I wanted him to do and be for me. I would tell him all the things he doesn't know about me. I would tell him that, even as a grown woman, I still look for him and need him. I would tell him about every superdaddy hero story that I created, and how he lived up to a few of them but failed me on so many. I would forgive him.

If I were a Black girl in love with myself . . .

I would whisper in my child's ear each night how beautiful, smart, creative, and amazing they are. I would not publicly shame or embarrass my child to reprimand them. I would not believe that beating or spanking is good for them. I would know that explaining right from wrong is better for their tiny soul and body. I would encourage them to disappoint others and me to remain true to their spirit, their soul, and themselves. I would tell my child that no matter what they did, I could never stop loving them. I would address in therapy all hidden jealousy, fear, and anger that their tiny presence stirs in me. I would know that these are my issues and are not the burden of my child to carry.

If I were a Black girl in love with myself . . .

I would cry often. Do big, public, ugly cries. Allow my tears to flow down my beautiful brown face. Cry because I'm hurt. Cry because I feel joy. Cry because I feel angry. I would not believe that I need to be given something to really cry about! I would know that it is safe to say I'm hurt, and it's okay for me to *not* have all the answers. I would know that I don't always need to be strong and to carry everyone's hurt and shame on my really small back. I would know it's okay to cry about the sexual secrets that I was told to keep as a young girl. It was not my fault. I give myself permission to cry in my car at a sad song on the radio.

If I were a Black girl in love with myself...

I would rest. That doesn't mean I'm lazy or lack ambition. I would light a candle. Read a book. (Perhaps, you can heal your life!) I would do nothing. Sit in my pajamas all day. Bake a chocolate cake and share it if I wish, but perhaps eat it all by myself! The world will not fall apart. I don't need to be completely drained to do it. The most loving act I can do is take some time for myself.

If I were a Black girl in love with myself...

I would have mini conversations with the Universe in my bed, in the shower, at my desk at work. I would thank the Universe for everything she has given me. I would ask the Universe to show me a path. I would trust that everything in my life is in divine and perfect order and that the Universe has a plan bigger for me than I could even imagine! I would dream beyond my circumstances!

If I were a Black girl in love with myself...

I would smile at every Black girl, regardless of how they respond to me. I would view them as allies and not my competition! I would cheer their victories as if they were my own! I would connect amazing Black women with each other and encourage them to get to know each other. I would offer to babysit their kids! I would have potlucks and sistah brunches. I would write empowering and loving messages on their Facebook pages. I would send them this piece! I would randomly tweet about how amazing they are. I would encourage my sistahs to be as smart as

Michelle, as outspoken as Whoopi, as creative as Shonda, as loving as Oprah, and as wise as Maya.

I would create safe places for them in my heart. I would send a Black girl some flowers, just because . . . and send myself some too!

Walk good, sistren.

Resources and Support

Mental Health/Therapy Resources

Black Female Therapists
www.blackfemaletherapists.com

Therapy for Black Girls
www.therapyforblackgirls.com

Sad Girls Club
www.sadgirlsclub.org

Talkspace
www.talkspace.com

National Suicide Prevention Lifeline
(800) 273-8255

Canadian Mental Health Resources

Mood Disorders Association of Ontario
www.mooddisorders.ca
(888) 486-8236

Affordable Therapy Network of Ontario
www.affordabletherapytoronto.com

Black Mental Health Canada
www.blackmentalhealth.ca
(289) 432-1377

Wellness/Exercise and Fitness

Black Girls RUN!
www.blackgirlsrun.com

Black Girl in OM
www.blackgirlinom.com

Black Girls Rock!
www.blackgirlsrock.com

GirlTrek
https://www.girltrek.org

OMNOIRE Retreats
www.omnoire.com
(646) 854-2214

LGBTQ Support

Zami Nobla
www.zaminobla.org
zaminobla@zaminobla.org
(404) 647-4754

National Black Justice Coalition
www.nbjc.org
(202) 285-4072

Kween Culture Initiative
(For transgender women of color)
www.kweenculture.com

Financial Support

Live Richer Academy
www.live-richer-academy.thinkific.com

Patrice Washington (financial guru)
www.patricewashington.com

The Frugal Feminista
www.thefrugalfeminista.com

Acknowledgments and Big Ups!

Universe/God, I knew in my darkest hours that you had a bigger plan for me. I knew that you had gifted me with my talent to share with others. Please continue to guide my steps. Thank you for every lesson.

My family, for always giving me something to write about. For always allowing me to share some of the most intimate parts of our lives. I love you. You make me better. You surround me with your loyalty and fierce love. You are the reason I'm able to laugh, love, and be myself at all times. I'm blessed to be loved by you.

To my son, "Kai Bear," You are the reason I got up from the floor. You are MY REASON. May you always continue to experience #blackboyjoy. May you know your mummy loves you so much.

My crew/di gyal dem! There are too many to name. So many of you came to hold me, support me, love me. Listen to me. Hold the baby. So many of you were the ones who told me to stop begging for love and go write my damn book! You were right! Trecia and Jackson, who picked me up from the bathroom floor that night and many other nights. A special shout out to Ashante Infantry who, when I was doubting myself and begging to be loved, told me, "Trey, I have faith this is not going to be your last chapter, or your last story. You are fucking damn TREY ANTHONY! Yu done know!"

Montie, you worked overtime. You watched the clock to remind me that I was late and needed to head out to go and write. You slept over so I could have more time to write. This book would not be possible if I did not have the peace of mind to know that you were looking after my beautiful baby while I typed away at my computer. I owe you the Porsche and it's coming... You cooked, you cleaned, you made me lunches to bring to my "writing room," you made my house a home. You love my son and you are more than just a "nanny." You are the damn co-pilot to my life. Kai and I love you so much.

Thanks to my girls, Jean and Cheryl, for your daily check-ins. They kept me afloat across the distance. Thanks to the team at Hay House, including the publisher Patty Gift and Allison Janice, who was my first contact with the publisher.

Melody/Yona/Dawn! The Black girl dream team! I have a Black editor, a Black publicist, a Black agent! Wow! You are the wind beneath my wings. My personal hype women. I know that you are invested in the success of this book as much as I am. Thank you for your support, love, and the belief that I could do this.

The glam squad who always make me look damn good! Danielle, Kiki, Shekeidra, Pris, I can't take a damn picture without you guys.

My amazing assistants, Nessa, Divine, and Keri—thank you for running my "little patty shop."

My fans/social media family. You have been there from day one. Always buying a ticket, sharing a flyer, buying a planner, sending me love and support. And now we finally have a book! Thank you. "Every forest was once a seed..."

To the bad-ass women who continue to inspire me from a distance: Oprah Winfrey, Michelle Obama, Shonda Rhimes, Serena Williams, India Arie, Bozoma Saint John, Sarah Jakes Roberts, Iyanla Vanzant, Lisa Nichols, Rachel Hollis, Marie Forleo. I'm watching you, taking notes, and continuing to send you mad love.

Much love to Jack Canfield and his team for his mentorship and support. I've studied your handbook. You are amazing!

Elayne Fluker of *Support Is Sexy*. Thank you for always being there and offering your insight and business guidance.

To everyone and anyone who has held me down, either in prayer, or by being there for me personally, or by supporting me, or by showing up. I love you. Thank you.

About the Author

Trey Anthony is infamous for doing a few foolish things for love, but she always learns her damn lesson! She has a bit of a potty mouth, but she's also an award-winning writer, motivational speaker, and relationship/life coach. She is the first Black woman in Canada to have a television series on a prime time net-  work, *'Da Kink in My Hair*. Her work includes the plays *'Da Kink in My Hair* and *How Black Mothers Say I Love You*. She is co-writing a feature film that is an adaption of her play *How Black Mothers Say I Love You*, which is supported by Telefilm Canada and Film Wales. Trey is a former writer for The Comedy Network, Global TV, and OWN, who has also written for the *Huffington Post*. Her TEDx Talk, "Coming Out of Your Box," made her Jamaican mom very proud!

Trey's life purpose is to empower Black women to live their best damn lives! She divides her time between Atlanta and Toronto. She is an adoption advocate and the proud momma bear to her son, Kai. She also a huge advocate for the rainbow community (you know who you are!).

In her spare time, she enjoys laughing at herself and eating vanilla cupcakes. Her favorite people include her nephew, Chance, and her therapist. She is an "okay" dancer but still dances likes no one is watching! She loves gangster rap and gospel music. Follow Trey on Instagram @blackgirlinlove and visit treyanthony.com to learn more about her.

Sis, Take Note!

Sis, Take Note!

_____

_____

_____

_____

_____

_____

_____

_____

_____

_____

_____

_____

_____

_____

Sis, Take Note!

Sis, Take Note!

_____

_____

_____

_____

_____

_____

_____

_____

_____

_____

_____

_____

_____

_____

Sis, Take Note!

Sis, Take Note!

_____

_____

_____

_____

_____

_____

_____

_____

_____

_____

_____

_____

_____

_____

Sis, Take Note!

_____

_____

_____

_____

_____

_____

_____

_____

_____

_____

_____

_____

_____

_____

Sis, Take Note!

_____

_____

_____

_____

_____

_____

_____

_____

_____

_____

_____

_____

_____

_____

Sis, Take Note!

_____

_____

_____

_____

_____

_____

_____

_____

_____

_____

_____

_____

_____

_____

Hay House Titles of Related Interest

We hope you enjoyed this Hay House book. If you'd like to receive our online catalog featuring additional information on Hay House books and products, or if you'd like to find out more about the Hay Foundation, please contact:

Hay House, Inc., P.O. Box 5100, Carlsbad, CA 92018-5100
(760) 431-7695 or (800) 654-5126
(760) 431-6948 (fax) or (800) 650-5115 (fax)
www.hayhouse.com® • www.hayfoundation.org

———

Published in Australia by: Hay House Australia Pty. Ltd.,
18/36 Ralph St., Alexandria NSW 2015
Phone: 612-9669-4299 • *Fax:* 612-9669-4144
www.hayhouse.com.au

Published in the United Kingdom by: Hay House UK, Ltd.,
The Sixth Floor, Watson House, 54 Baker Street, London W1U 7BU
Phone: +44 (0)20 3927 7290 • *Fax:* +44 (0)20 3927 7291
www.hayhouse.co.uk

Published in India by: Hay House Publishers India,
Muskaan Complex, Plot No. 3, B-2, Vasant Kunj, New Delhi 110 070
Phone: 91-11-4176-1620 • *Fax:* 91-11-4176-1630
www.hayhouse.co.in

———

<u>Access New Knowledge.</u>
<u>Anytime. Anywhere.</u>

Learn and evolve at your own pace
with the world's leading experts.

www.hayhouseU.com